P9-DMY-046

Washington, D.C.

A Pictorial Celebration

Jeanne Fogle

Photography by Elan Penn

Sterling Publishing Co., Inc.
New York

Design and layout: Michel Opatowski
Copyedited by Jennifer E. Sigler

Library of Congress Cataloging-in-Publication Data Available

18 17 16 15 14 13

Published by Sterling Publishing Co., Inc.
387 Park Avenue South, New York, NY 10016

Distributed in Canada by Sterling Publishing
℅ Canadian Manda Group, 165 Dufferin Street
Toronto, Ontario, Canada M6K 3H6
Distributed in the United Kingdom by GMC Distribution Services
Castle Place, 166 High Street, Lewes, East Sussex, England BN7 1XU
Distributed in Australia by Capricorn Link (Australia) Pty. Ltd.
P.O. Box 704, Windsor, NSW 2756, Australia

Printed in China

Sterling ISBN-13: 978-1-4027-1527-3
ISBN-10: 1-4027-1527-7

Contents

Washington: A Chosen City

Washington wasn't born beautiful. The capital city on the Potomac, carefully conceived and meticulously planned, has taken more than two centuries to build. And yet the history of the dream city continues to be made.

Congress created Washington by authorizing the Residence Act of 1790. The nation's capital had to be a separate territory, not part of any city or state, not more than a hundred square miles in size, and centrally located among the 13 states. To reach a compromise, a vote was held in Congress and a site on the Potomac River won favor.

George Washington accepted full responsibility for executing congressional directives for the new city. He chose the exact location—at the highest navigable point on the river. Two states, Maryland and Virginia, were both to cede land, including two busy commercial port cities. George Washington believed that this location would serve to strengthen the Union politically and economically.

The great commission of creating a city worthy of the Nation was assigned to a visionary French engineer, Pierre (Peter) L'Enfant, who had served in the Continental Army under General Washington. In a letter from 1789, he boasts of his ambition to be a useful citizen and to acquire a reputation by sharing in the founding of "a city which is to become the Capital of this vast Empire."

L'Enfant surveyed the site and chose two hills, on which he placed the "Congress' House" (the Capitol) and the "President's Palace" (the White House). He carefully arranged the streets in a grid: north/south were numbered; east/west were lettered. He then added wide, radiating, diagonal avenues named after the states, which overlapped the grid and created unusually shaped property lots: some were intended as parks; others, when built upon, would add immense interest to the architecture of the city.

Reveling in the details of his plan, L'Enfant visualized picturesque parks, circles, and squares scattered throughout the city, filled with fountains, statues, gardens, and shade trees. He envisioned prominently placed, noble government buildings, fancy foreign embassies, and fine private residences. As the wealth of the country increased, it would be reflected in future improvements to the capital, an expectation that L'Enfant expressed unambiguously: "A plan should be drawn on such a scale as to leave room for . . . aggrandizement and embellishment . . . [and] must leave to posterity a grand idea of the patriotic interest which promoted it."

What's in a Name: Why Washington, D.C.?

Originally, the Federal City might have been called Washington, T.C. In 1791 the first city commissioners unanimously agreed to name the Federal City for George Washington, and the surrounding "territory" for Christopher Columbus, to honor the three hundredth anniversary of his discovery of the New World. "Columbus" was changed to "Columbia," and "Territory" was replaced with the more provincial term "District." George Washington, however, continued to call it "the Federal City."

In the old District of Columbia, there were three cities: Washington, the Federal City; Georgetown, formerly a port in Maryland; and Alexandria, formerly a port in Virginia. The balance of the land ceded by Maryland was Washington County, and the land ceded by Virginia was called Alexandria County.

In 1846 the Alexandrians requested that their portion of the District of Columbia be retroceded to Virginia. Congress obliged, thereby reducing the federal territory to 70 square miles of land on the northern side of the Potomac.

Following the Civil War, the boundaries of the city of Washington were expanded to incorporate both Georgetown and Washington County. "Washington" and "District of Columbia" are two names that now refer to the same place.

Three Branches of Government: Makers, Executers, and Interprters of the Law

Washington was created for the purpose of properly accommodating the federal government. Members of Congress wanted control over the place where they worked. They also wanted to put an end to their exasperating nomadic existence: in the 15 years prior to moving to Washington, Congress had convened in eight different cities located in four different states, always meeting in shared or borrowed buildings.

Congress allotted ten years, from 1790 to 1800, for the creation of the new Federal City. Construction began on the White House in 1792, and on the Capitol a year later. At the time, no separate structure was built for the Supreme Court, which held its sessions in temporary quarters in the Capitol for 134 years. The four government departments of State, War, Navy, and Treasury moved into two fine brick buildings that flanked the White House. The Post Office and Patent Office were located in a building originally constructed as a hotel.

The government workforce was small in 1800: there were 32 senators and 106 representatives, the president and vice president, six Supreme Court justices, four Cabinet secretaries, the U.S. postmaster, and 131 government clerks. In 1801 the entire population of Washington was counted at 3,244.

The federal government, driven by its desire to convey a sense of permanency, began building immense, impressive, columned and pedimented stone structures for itself. In the 1830s, construction was started simultaneously on the neoclassical Treasury Department, Patent Office, and Post Office; these buildings would not be completed, however, for another 30 years.

After the Civil War, the largest government office building in the world (at the time) was erected next to the White House. Designed in the ornamental Second Empire architectural style, it housed the Departments of State, War, and Navy. By the 1930s, neoclassical style architecture was revived in the designs of the imposing Federal Triangle buildings that lined Pennsylvania Avenue.

Today, the city of Washington supports hundreds of thousands of government workers, many of whom perform their official duties in these magnificent historic structures. The size and scale of these noble federal buildings serve to reinforce their relationship to the nation—not just the city—and they

Capitol Building, 1846. Courtesy of the Frances Loeb Library, Harvard Design School.

convey a sense of public pride and a firm belief in the future.

In Memory of the Country's Greatest Leaders: Presidential Memorials

Partly by plan, partly by luck and happenstance were the nation's great presidential memorials brought into existence. The first was the Washington Monument, which stood uncompleted for 26 years. Its beauty lies in its simplicity, its grandeur, and in its imposing height. Designed to be the tallest masonry structure in the world, the monument devolved into a simple obelisk when a lack of funds forced the elimination of the highly ornate temple designed to encircle the base.

The Washington Monument is visible from almost any point in the city, serving as a constant reminder of the man who set the standards for the office of the presidency, who is called "the Father of our Country," and for whom the nation's capital is named. The view in any direction from the Washington Monument is inspirational: to the east is the Capitol; to the north, the White House; to the west, the Lincoln Memorial; and to the south, the Thomas Jefferson Memorial.

Controversy, squabbling, and protests accompanied the creation of the beloved Lincoln and Jef-

Lincoln Memorial and basin, 1930, West Potomac Park (west end of the Mall). Courtesy of the Frances Loeb Library, Harvard Design School.

ferson Memorials. Speaker of the House Joe Cannon warned that no one would ever visit a memorial to Lincoln if it were built in "that God-forsaken swamp." Construction of the Jefferson Memorial was almost halted before it began when ladies chained themselves to the cherry blossom trees at the site to save them from imminent destruction; in the resulting compromise, ten new trees were planted for each one that was cut down. Architectural critics of the time despised the memorial's classical design, nicknaming it "Jefferson's Muffin."

A major memorial was not built for President Franklin Delano Roosevelt until 50 years after his death. Andrew Jackson's statue was a labor of love by the artist, who had to construct his own foundry in which to cast it. President Garfield's monument was quickly erected as the result of an outpouring of grief over his assassination. One of John F. Kennedy's many memorials, a performing arts center, was also built in mourning, but with the intention of bringing great joy to those who visit it.

Of all of Washington's memorials, the most prominent are those that pay tribute to the nation's great leaders, and the best-loved are those dedicated to presidents, whether in the form of temples, statues, buildings, or grand parks.

Sentinels of Freedom: Our National Memorials

"Freedom is Not Free." This simple phrase, inscribed on the wall of the Korean War Veterans Memorial, is a constant reminder of how dear and how costly our freedom is. Two centuries before this memorial was dedicated, the city's planner, L'Enfant, was concerned about the country's future defense: "How and upon what foundations could it be supposed that America will have nothing to fear? . . . A neutral power must be ready for war, and his [sic] trade depends on the means of protecting and making his colors respected."

Washington abounds with war memorials, each of them unique but all telling a similar story. No memorial better portrays patriotism, courage, and devotion to country than the United States Marine Corps War Memorial (the Iwo Jima Memorial)—first captured in a photograph and later in bronze—with its scene of six soldiers struggling to raise a huge American flag. The statue of the lone sailor stands proud and vigilant at the United States Navy Memorial, embodying the personal sacrifices that servicemen and -women endure away from home. The emotional reality of war is encapsulated in the Vietnam Veterans Memorial through "the power of a name"—of more than 58,000 names, that is—of those who died in the war or are still missing.

Arlington National Cemetery, with its seemingly endless rows of white marble headstones lined up like soldiers in formation, is the most constant reminder of the price of freedom. As the final resting place of two presidents; three unknown soldiers; the city's planner, Pierre L'Enfant; and nearly 200,000 servicemen and -women, it is a place of pilgrimage and the nation's most hallowed ground.

Freedom carries with it many responsibilities, including the responsibility not to forget the past. Memorials embody our collective memory, serving as sentinels of freedom and visual reminders of the cost of securing "the Blessing of Liberty to ourselves and our Posterity."

Keepers of History: Protecting Our Past

A few chosen Washington organizations, institutions, and government entities have become the repositories of the nation's invaluable documents and priceless historical objects. Premier among them is the Library of Congress, where each working day 7,000 new items are added to the Library's collection. Second only to the Library is the National Archives, which has been called "the Depository of the Priceless." Within its walls are protected, preserved, and permanently displayed this country's original Charters of Freedom.

One of the world's greatest privately established scientific foundations, the Smithsonian Institution, strives to collect, document, and exhibit millions of objects relating to nearly every aspect of history, science, art, technology, and American life and culture both past and present.

Geographers, cartographers, explorers, and geologists have found assistance, encouragement, and recognition for their work through the National Geographic Society. In its world-famous magazine, the world has been dissected, described, and explained for scientists and laymen alike.

Guardians of Art and Sculpture: Galleries and Gardens

Many great cities are best known for their artists, but Washington is known for its collectors. Washingtonian William Wilson Corcoran set a trend when he established the first art gallery in the city: the Corcoran Gallery of Art is now one of the largest and oldest privately operated art museums in the nation.

Duncan Phillips opened the first museum in the United States dedicated to modern art and its origins. Andrew W. Mellon and his children, Paul and Alisa, generously endowed the National Gallery of Art with one of the world's finest collections of Western European and American art.

The Smithsonian's collection of art has been immensely enhanced through many generous, individual bequests: from Charles Lang Freer, who set the standards for Asian art collections; Arthur M. Sackler, who collected art as a biologist in order to understand different societies; and from Joseph Hirshhorn, who collected modern art and sculpture with a passion. Also part of the Smithsonian are special galleries dedicated specifically to the study of African art, American art, American crafts, and American historical portraits.

To study art is to study people, whether through portraits, collected art objects, or the collectors themselves. As Duncan Phillips explained, they sought to bring us through their personal philanthropy "into the land of artists' dreams."

Sacred Structures: Saving Our Souls

At first glance Washington may not seem like a religious place, but houses of worship abound. Little St. John's Episcopal Church, across from the White House, has always been called the "Church of the Presidents." Nearly all the presidents claim to have worshiped there at least once. From this church's congregation arose the grand idea to create a church for the nation, an idea that resulted in the establishment of the Washington National Cathedral, an Episcopal church known as "a house of prayer for all peoples" and a place to be openly used in times of national celebration or mourning.

Across town from the Cathedral is the largest Catholic church in the western hemisphere, the Basilica of the National Shrine of the Immaculate Conception, dedicated to Mary and the glory of womanhood. In the heart of downtown is the old

United States Treasury Building, circa 1900. Courtesy of the Frances Loeb Library, Harvard Design School.

Cathedral of St. Matthew the Apostle, where President Kennedy's funeral mass was held. Because St. Matthew is the patron saint of civil servants, the famous "Red Mass" is celebrated here each year in October to request guidance for civil servants in their professional conduct. The Constitution separates church and state, but government workers are always welcome at any of Washington's sacred structures.

Outdoor Beauty: Parks and Gardens

Washington has been called a "City of Trees" and might very well be the best-shaded city in America. The city does boast a tremendous variety in species of trees, reflecting the diversity of its history, residents, architects, and its politics. Commemorative trees have been planted by congressmen, diplomats, and architects to hide their less successful building designs.

Some areas in Washington have been allowed to remain unchanged. Chief among them is Rock Creek Park, which runs through the heart of the city. Planned gardens, like those belonging to the Smithsonian Institution or the U.S. Botanic Garden, have a mission to both delight and educate. The formal gardens of Dumbarton Oaks Estate were designed to overwhelm. Little informal gardens—tended or "au naturel"—abound, both in residential areas and downtown.

L'Enfant intended that there be an abundance of open space in the city for gardens, fountains, and trees. For two hundred years, visionary urban planners and the country's greatest landscape architects have lavished their expertise on the open spaces of Washington, trying to follow L'Enfant's dream and to interpret and enhance his vision. The result is a city of unmatched beauty.

Historic Preservation: Saving Our Past

The first successful preservation effort in Washington was undertaken by the American Institute of Architects when it bought and restored the Octagon House, the city's first privately built mansion. In the 1960s, ownership of the grand old Washington home of former president Woodrow Wilson was transferred to the National Trust for Historic Preservation for future safekeeping, and it was opened to the public.

A few historic Washington homes have been generously endowed and preserved through the concerted efforts of their owners. Tudor Place, home of Martha Washington's granddaughter, was preserved by her descendants, and Hillwood was endowed by its owner, called "the American Heiress."

The government was responsible for inadvertently saving and ultimately restoring Ford's Theatre, where President Lincoln was shot.

Local historians, preservationists, and occasionally politicians have become involved in battles to preserve historic government buildings from eminent destruction, among them the Old Post Office, the Old Pension Building, and Union Station. As new development encroaches on the old Washington neighborhoods, the war against history escalates. Preserving our past is becoming a priority for current residents and hopefully will be a consideration for future generations as well.

Outdoor Sculpture: Memorials to Heroes and Peacemakers

Statues of both U.S. and foreign military heroes pose on horseback or stand atop their pedestals in public parks. Great philosophers, scientists, teachers, and poets are represented in sculptural form across the city. Altogether, hundreds of memorials remind passersby of the country's history and purpose while adding marvelous beauty to the cityscape.

Many circles and parks in Washington were renamed after the Civil War to honor Union army and navy heroes, among them General Sheridan, Major General Logan, Admiral Farragut, and General Grant.

Foreign military heroes who contributed to America's victory in the Revolutionary War are honored with statues placed in Lafayette Square. Statues of Hispanic heroes, near the Organization of American States building, pay tribute to a spirit of international goodwill and celebrate two centuries of friendship between the United States and the nations of Latin America.

Exceptional individuals who have had great influence across the nation or throughout the world are honored as well: Martin Luther King Jr., George Mason, Daniel Webster, Mary McLeod Bethune, Albert Einstein, and Mahatma Gandhi are all commemorated in the capital.

Washington is a city of statues and memorials. Hundreds—both great and small—have been dedicated around the city and many more are in the planning, because, as a nation, we don't want our history to be forgotten.

Unusual Statues: Personal Expression

Private organizations and individuals have donated numerous works of art in Washington; some are wonderfully unusual, others have a great story to tell. Among the memorials with a message are the Temperance Fountain, erected to admonish against the consumption of alcoholic beverages, and the Titanic Memorial, honoring the courage of those who chose to go down with the sinking of the great ocean liner so that women and children might be saved.

Public sculpture has the power to inspire and one brilliant piece of funeral statuary in Rock Creek Cemetery has been an inspiration to many: the Adams Memorial, known as "Peace" or "Grief," is considered a masterpiece.

Higher Education: A City of Learning

Washington boasts that its residents are amongst the best educated in the country. The city is a mecca of learning: seven universities are located in Washington, and individual government departments, organizations, institutions, and museums also offer a variety of educational courses in the city.

To have a great national university built in the Federal City was one of George Washington's greatest desires. Columbian College was chartered in 1820 and later changed its name to the George Washington University.

Georgetown University, the first Catholic academic institution established in the United States, opened a year before Congress voted to create the District of Columbia. Howard University was chartered after the Civil War in response to the need for higher education, predominately for freedmen living in the nation's capital. It is the oldest black college in America.

"Establish the law for educating the common people," wrote Thomas Jefferson, who maintained throughout his life that self-government could only work if the governed were educated.

Perhaps, Washington wasn't born beautiful, but 200 years of devoted attention have made the Nation's Capital a uniquely attractive city and a premier showcase of natural and man-made beauty among the cities of the world. L'Enfant's vision for the Federal City was so great that its realization has taken generations to achieve, and the work continues.

Three Branches of Government: Makers, Executers, and Interpreters of the Law

The Capitol

The Capitol is "the first temple dedicated to the sovereignty of the people," wrote Thomas Jefferson. He envisioned a building that would be simple, noble, and beautiful. In 1792 a contest was held for the design of the Capitol. The winning plan was submitted by Dr. William Thornton, a man of independent means and many talents who made Washington his home. He later designed two of the most beautiful houses in the city, Octagon House and Tudor Place.

Construction of the Capitol began in 1793. Still unfinished 21 years later, it was gutted by fire when British soldiers responded to the alleged command of Admiral George Cockburn to "burn this harbor of Yankee democracy." Congress evacuated the city during the British invasion; when they returned, all they found left standing of the Capitol were its blackened exterior walls.

They decided to rebuild and hired Benjamin Henry Latrobe, the architect of Decatur House and St. John's Church on Lafayette Square. In redesigning the Capitol, Latrobe created some of the most beautiful neoclassical interiors in America, including the Old Supreme Court Chamber with its vaulted ceiling, the stately Old House Chamber, and the magnificent Old Senate Chamber where Webster, Calhoun, and Clay eloquently debated the future of the nation.

By 1828 the Capitol's low stone dome was enclosed by a copper-clad, wooden-frame cover designed by Charles Bullfinch. Thirty years later, when the Capitol was expanded to include the new north wing for the Senate and the south wing for the House of Representatives, a tall, innovative cast-iron dome replaced the original one, crowned with Thomas Crawford's symbolic statue Freedom.

Beneath the great iron dome, in the concave ceiling over the Rotunda, is the impressive allegorical fresco that glorifies George Washington. The

Previous page: The Capitol.

fresco's artist, Italian-born U.S. patriot Constantino Brumidi, dedicated the last 25 years of his life to creating many of the Capitol's decorative mural paintings. "My one ambition and my daily prayer," he confessed, "is that I may live long enough to make beautiful the Capitol of the one country on earth in which there is liberty."

Architectural modifications continue to be made to the Capitol, most recently with the construction of a monumental Visitor Center. For more than two centuries, numerous architects have dedicated their talents to the evolving design of the Capitol, resulting in the most magnificent structure in Washington. And yet, the question posed by a senator returning to Washington after the Civil War will probably be echoed by generations to come: "How's the Capitol? Is it finished?"

Thomas Jefferson statue
by P. J. David d'Angers, 1833,
the Capitol Rotunda.

The White House

"The White House is built as much of personalities as of stone," wrote William Seale in his two-volume chronicle, *The President's House*. In 1791 the city's planner, Pierre L'Enfant, envisioned a "President's Palace" 700 feet long and situated on a lofty ridge amid an elaborately landscaped "President's Park." George Washington, though a devotee of L'Enfant's plan, was also a practical man who significantly diminished the size of the house and then requested that all of the city's new public buildings be made appropriate for "the ages to come."

Thomas Jefferson suggested holding a national competition for the plan of the president's house. Nine imaginative, somewhat eccentric entries were submitted. An accomplished Irish-born, South Carolinian architect, James Hoban, entered the competition with President Washington's encouragement. By 1792 construction had begun on Hoban's winning design for the new Federal City's first federal building, which would later be named the White House.

George Washington was the only president never to live in the White House. When John Adams arrived, the house itself was unfinished and unfurnished, but the front yard was full of workmen's sheds and brickyard kilns, a deserted farmhouse, a family cemetery, and a racetrack that cut across a corner of the lawn. Thomas Jefferson moved in with innumerable ideas for home improvements, the first of which was to replace the outdoor wooden privy with

The Blue Room, courtesy of the White House Historical Association. Photo by Bruce White.

two indoor water closets. He landscaped the grounds and greatly enriched the interior chambers.

The White House was burned by the British in 1814, then rebuilt under President Madison and finely furnished under President Monroe. Each president and first lady has left their imprint on the White House and, collectively, their contributions have created the best-known, best-loved home in America.

In turn, the White House has left its mark on its residents: Jefferson referred to his presidency as a "splendid misery," Jackson compared it to "dignified slavery," and Theodore Roosevelt called it a "glorious burden." It was John Adams, however, on his first evening alone in the White House, who offered a "prayer" that is now carved into the State Dining Room's marble mantle for all future presidents to see: "I pray Heaven to bestow the best of blessings on this house, and on all that shall hereafter inhabit it. May none but honest and wise men ever rule under this roof !"

The Supreme Court of the United States

"The Court of Last Resort" is a nickname conferred upon the Supreme Court of the United States. The justices of this court form the most powerful tribunal in the world. For 134 years, however, they had no building in which to meet. They borrowed space in hand-me-down chambers in the Capitol that served as their temporary courtrooms, and their offices were in their homes.

In 1928 the indomitable Chief Justice William Howard Taft, who had been president two decades earlier, urged that a permanent home for the Court be found. Within just a few years, a dazzling, new, white marble edifice for the Supreme Court was built, but it so overwhelmed several of the justices that they were reluctant to vacate their familiar, modest old courtroom in the Capitol. One justice observed, "We will look like nine black beetles in the temple of Karnak."

"Equal Justice Under Law" is boldly inscribed on the pediment over the entrance to the Supreme Court. The building was designed by architect Cass Gilbert, and because it was constructed during the Great Depression the $5 million allotted budget proved excessive: the government, try as it might, seemed unable to spend it all. In 1935, after completing and fully furnishing the new building, $94,000 was returned to the U.S. Treasury.

Neither William Howard Taft nor architect Cass Gilbert were alive when the Supreme Court building was dedicated. However, both are memorialized—wearing Roman-style togas—in the sculpted pediment over the entry: Taft is the reclining figure on the far left and Cass Gilbert is two figures to his right. The artist who sculpted the pediment, Robert Aiken, carved his own likeness onto the face of the next-to-the-last figure on the right.

Turtles are among the many animal symbols used as ornamentation at the Supreme Court. Cast into the bases of the bronze lampposts are turtles pulling in four different directions. A turtle and rabbit are carved at opposite ends of the marble pediment on the back of the building, representing the characters in Aesop's fable "The Hare and the Tortoise." The race was won by the tortoise because, though he was slow, he was steady in his pursuit—and so the turtle has come to embody the "slow but steady progress" of justice.

EQUAL JUSTI

UNDER · LAW ·

Federal Bureaucracy: The Government at Work

United States Treasury Building

In its early years, fires and scandals plagued the Treasury Department. The first building housing the Treasury was burned by the British in 1814. Less than twenty years later, a second, identical building was destroyed by fire. The third building, however, proved to be fireproof. Designed in the neoclassical style, its eastern facade featured a monumental sandstone colonnade 466 feet long. By the 1860s, north, south, and west wings were added, built of gray granite from Maine, and granite columns later replaced the old sandstone ones.

The primary function of the Treasury Department is the management of money. Public trust in the Treasury was first put to the test in 1777 when, to help finance the Revolutionary War, the Continental Congress printed two million bills of credit. Unfortunately these Continental Dollars devalued so rapidly that soon they were worthless, provoking the expression "not worth a Continental."

First Secretary of the Treasury, Alexander Hamilton, restored the citizens' confidence by establishing a national bank, national currency, and the U.S. Mint. He also left a national debt of $14 million. Albert Gallatin succeeded Hamilton as secretary and not only paid off the debt but created the nation's first surplus. Statues of both men stand on opposite sides of the Treasury Building.

During the Civil War, scores of women who were considered needy but well-born were hired at the Treasury Department. Many later testified that they received their jobs because they yielded to the embraces of certain gentlemen.

President Grant's first inaugural ball was held in the Treasury's elegant Cash Room, which became so overcrowded that ladies began to faint and others just "subsided in ungraceful groups on the floor," in the words of Horace Greeley. A riot nearly ensued when the hungry crowd was refused a promised dinner. Departing guests discovered that their cloaks had been stacked in disorderly piles; many grabbed any wrap they could find, leaving others to search in vain or do without.

The Cash Room, which opened in 1869, was the last major construction project at the Treasury. Often called the costliest room in the world, with walls lined in seven types of marble it was clearly designed to exude confidence. The Cash Room's vault once held millions of dollars and for more than a century workers came there to cash their paychecks, to exchange old money for new, and to buy U.S. Treasury Bonds. Architect Alfred Mullett claimed that the room was "emblematic of the dignity of the nation and the stability of its credit," just as, on a grander scale, the Treasury Building stands as the symbol of America's financial dealings with the world.

Previous page: Federal Triangle.

Bureau of Engraving and Printing

Every day the Bureau of Engraving and Printing prints up to $696 million in U.S. paper currency. "Paper" money isn't really made of paper, though. Prior to World War I, bills were printed on silk; today's bills are 75 percent cotton and 25 percent linen. Though a bill can survive about 4,000 backward-forward folds before tearing and can remain in circulation for about 18 months, replacement bills still account for 95 percent of all the money that is printed.

First issued in Massachusetts in 1690, paper money is considered an American invention. In colonial days, the British government passed a series of bans against the issuance and export of coins and paper currency, which hindered American life and commerce—an injustice that contributed to the outbreak of the Revolutionary War. Congress supported the war financially by issuing the Continental Dollar—unfortunately, a miserable failure. Until the Civil War, "folding money" as currency was generally rejected in favor of coins.

In the 1870s, the U.S. Treasury assumed the task of printing all government-issued currency, stamps, and bonds. It was at this time that a red-brick, castle-style building was constructed not far from the Washington Monument—solely for the purpose of printing money. By 1914 the Bureau of Engraving and Printing moved to a new, neoclassical, limestone building nearby, where the majority of the nation's currency is still printed. Visitors to the Bureau of Engraving and Printing are often told that even if they have never been there before, their money has.

Eisenhower Executive Office Building

(The Old State, War, and Navy Office Building)

"It is the ugliest building in America," commented Mark Twain, referring to the State, War, and Navy Building. Completed in 1888, the Navy vacated the reviled edifice by 1918, the War Department left in 1938, and the State Department moved out in 1947. The empty offices, however, were quickly filled with White House staff. When possession of the building was transferred to the Executive Office of the President in 1949, Harry Truman disparagingly remarked that it was "the greatest monstrosity in America."

Beginning in 1800 the Treasury, State, War, and Navy Departments were located in buildings next to the White House. By 1866 the new Building for the Treasury was completed and the adjoining structure housing the Department of State was demolished, forcing the employees to relocate into temporary quarters at the D.C. Orphan Asylum. At the same time, the War and Navy Buildings had become overcrowded and outdated and needed to be torn down and replaced. Controversy over the State, War, and Navy Building began long before it was built. Inspired by the new architectural trends popular in Paris, architect Alfred Mullett designed a modern, Second Empire–style structure in 1871 that severely contrasted with the nearby Greek Revival–style Treasury Department. By the time Mullett's building was completed 17 years later, the architectural style was embarrassingly old-fashioned. Although Secretary of State John Hay proclaimed the building "Mr. Mullett's masterpiece," his friend Henry Adams called it "Mr. Mullett's architectural infant asylum!"

The State, War, and Navy Building was indisputably the largest granite structure in the world, as well as the biggest office building in America. The base walls are 4½ feet thick; interior decorations are of cast iron or plaster; the 553 rooms have 1,572 windows and 1,314 interior doors, each with fancy brass doorknobs bearing the insignias of the State, War, or Navy Departments.

The two miles of corridors were once kept polished by an army of cleaning women riding through the hallways on bicycles with mops attached to the back. The 4,000 shiny, cast-bronze staircase balusters reminded one worker of "a golden stairway to heaven." In defending the building's virtues, another admirer diplomatically explained: "She has all the requisites of a great aunt. She is neither very pretty nor elegant, but she has enduring qualities of character."

Federal Triangle

"Washington is not only the nation's capital, it is the symbol of America," proclaimed President Herbert Hoover in 1929. "By its dignity and architectural inspiration we stimulate pride in our country." Hoover spoke these words at the dedication of the Department of Commerce Building, the first in a series of planned government office buildings erected on an enormous, triangular-shaped piece of property between the Capitol and the White House.

Between 1926 and 1937 the federal government undertook a mammoth building project for the purpose of adequately accommodating the enormous increase of government workers who had flocked to Washington during and after World War I. The "Federal Triangle Project" consisted of seven monumental buildings for the Departments of Commerce and Justice, the Labor-Interstate Commerce Commission, the Federal Trade Commission, the Bureau of Internal Revenue, the Post Office, and the National Archives. The new federal office buildings paid tribute to the principles of L'Enfant's original city plan, maintaining the classical architectural tradition initiated by the designers of the White House and the Capitol.

The Federal Triangle's architects were masters of the popular École des Beaux Arts style taught in Paris, a style in which academic, architectural sculpture and embellishments are intrinsic to the building's design, adding not just beauty but also a sense of the function of the structure. The allegorical sculptures on the buildings' exteriors represent such themes as "Liberty of Worship," "Voice of Reason," "Spirit of Civilization and Progress," and philosophies like "Past Is Prologue." The Federal Triangle buildings proudly display more architectural sculpture—112 masterworks by forty-seven artists—than can be found in most U.S. cities.

Each building is unique, but together they form a unified whole, fulfilling the original ideal promoted in the early part of the twentieth century by Treasury Secretary Andrew W. Mellon and the Commission of Fine Arts to create "a lasting inspiration and collective architectural symbol of the capital."

In Memory of the Country's Greatest Leaders: Presidential Memorials

Washington Monument

George Washington was universally loved and revered throughout the late eighteenth and nineteenth centuries, but getting a monument built in his honor was not easy. Congress first proposed erecting an equestrian statue to Washington even before he was president, but 70 years passed before it was finally cast. After he died, Congress had a crypt built in the Capitol for Washington's remains; but in accordance with his family's wishes and his will, he was buried at Mount Vernon.

In anticipation of the 1832 centennial celebration of the first president's birth, Congress commissioned a marble statue of Washington. The sculptor, Horatio Greenough, portrayed him in a Zeus-like fashion, bare-chested, seated with one arm raised, draped in a toga, and wearing sandals. The public was outraged at the near-naked statue of Washington, and it was quickly relocated from inside the Capitol to outside, where it remained for 60 years. The statue was given to the Smithsonian Institution

The George Washington statue by Horatio Greenough, 1841, Smithsonian National Museum of American History.

Previous page: Thomas Jefferson Memorial.

Equestrian statue of Washington by Clark Mills, 1860. Washington Circle.

and put in storage for another 60 years before finally being permanently displayed in the Smithsonian National Museum of American History.

In the 1830s, a private organization held a design competition for the grandest of the monuments to George Washington, which would be placed on a site located west of the Capitol and south of the White House. Robert Mills won the contest with his drawing of a square obelisk-like shaft. Standing at nearly one-tenth of a mile high, it was to be surrounded by a 100-foot tall, circular, columned temple decorated with heroic figures, including a colossal toga-clad statue of Washington seated in a chariot and driving a team of four horses.

Construction began after 15 years of fund-raising, only to be stopped 6 years later, when the funds were exhausted and the shaft was only one-third completed. States were invited to make contributions, and Alabama, instead of sending money, sent an inscribed block of native stone to be placed inside the monument near the stairway, for all to see. Mimicking the gesture, major cities, private societies, foreign governments, and the Pope all sent commemorative stones. When the Pope's stone was stolen, however, the construction was halted.

Meanwhile, in the 1850s, Congress paid artist Clark Mills (no relation to Robert Mills) to finally create an equestrian statue of General Washington. At first, it was suggested the statue be placed near the uncompleted Washington Monument. Instead, it was erected in the center of Washington Circle, and it portrays the General leading the surprise attack against the British at Trenton.

Another 25 years passed before Congress appropriated funds to complete the Washington Monument. By that time, Robert Mills' design was reduced to a simple, majestic 555-foot-tall obelisk, without a temple. On February 21, 1885, a ceremony was held for the placement of the "capstone," a 100-ounce aluminum pyramid inscribed with the phrase: *Laus Deo* ("God be praised"). President Chester A. Arthur then solemnly dedicated the world's tallest masonry structure "to the immortal name and memory of George Washington."

Mount Vernon.

Thomas Jefferson Memorial

Complex and multifaceted, Thomas Jefferson is considered a hero by laymen and scholars alike. Historian Ken Burns wrote about Jefferson: "A hero is not perfect . . . indeed, what makes a hero interesting are the inner negotiations between that person's great strengths and obvious, inevitable weaknesses."

President Franklin D. Roosevelt greatly admired Jefferson and urged that a memorial be erected for him. The result was the last of the great beaux-arts marble monuments in Washington. Designed by architect John Russell Pope in the 1930s, it was situated on the Tidal Basin directly south of, and in view of, the White House. The memorial is a fitting architectural tribute to Jefferson, modeled after his favorite building: the Pantheon in Rome. Jefferson was an accomplished architect who used the proportions of the Pantheon to design his home, Monticello, as well as the rotunda of the University of Virginia.

Inside the memorial, Jefferson's statue by artist Rudolph Evans portrays him at the age of 43 as an author and political philosopher holding a scrolled document, and as a diplomat wearing the coat that was a gift from the Polish General Thaddeus Kosciusko. Jefferson thought of himself as a farmer, inventor, and scholar. Evans acknowledged this in subtle carvings on the statue's base: ears of corn, leaves of tobacco, an improved plow, and a stack of books.

Jefferson's true spirit has been captured in the monument's inscriptions, including quotes from the Declaration of Independence, from the Virginia Statute for Religious Freedom, and from Jefferson's own writings and correspondences—which are just as relevant today as they were at the time they were written. Jefferson's words to Benjamin Rush are inscribed around the inside collar of the dome: "I have sworn upon the altar of God eternal hostility against every form of tyranny over the mind of man."

FORM OF TY
NNY
GAVE US
ES OF A
WE HAVE
AT THESE
F GOD?
OUNTRY
IS JUST,
EEP FOR-
MASTER
OTHING
IN THE
THESE
ABLISH
OMMON
SINESS
ND ON

One hundred years before the Jefferson Memorial was dedicated, a statue depicting Jefferson as founding father, political philosopher, and author was placed in the Capitol. Parisian artist Pierre-Jean David d'Angers sculpted Jefferson holding a quill pen in his right hand and a copy of the Declaration of Independence in his left. The statue was a gift from the Jewish Captain Uriah P. Levy, who explained that he gave it in appreciation of Jefferson's "determined stand on the side of religious liberty." President Polk relocated it to the front lawn of the White House, making it the only presidential statue ever to stand there. Years later it was returned to the Capitol's Rotunda.

Jefferson served his country as emissary to France, the first secretary of state, the second vice president, and the third president, and he established the Library of Congress by selling the government his personal library of 6,487 books. Yet from all his accomplishments, Jefferson singled out just a few for which he hoped to be remembered: "Author of the Declaration of American Independence, of the Statute of Virginia for Religious Freedom, and Father of the University of Virginia. By these, as testaments that I have lived, I wish most to be remembered."

On July 4, 1826, the fiftieth anniversary of the signing of the Declaration of Independence, both Thomas Jefferson and John Adams died. Adams' last words were prophetic: "Jefferson lives." Through his words and thoughts, he lives on.

"In this temple, as in the hearts of the people for whom he saved the Union, the memory of Abraham Lincoln is enshrined forever." Composed almost as an afterthought by art critic Royall Cortissoz, this inscription was placed on the wall behind and above the statue of Lincoln in the Lincoln Memorial.

The plans for a memorial to Lincoln were debated in Congress for nearly half a century. In 1912 a design by architect Henry Bacon was selected: a marble parthenon surrounded by 36 columns, one for each of the 36 states in the Union at the Civil War's end. Inscribed in the memorial's walls are Lincoln's most famous speeches: the Gettysburg Address and his second inaugural address.

Artist Daniel Chester French, the premier sculptor of the time, was chosen to design the colossal 19-foot-tall statue of Lincoln seated. Carved of Georgian white marble and raised up high on a marble pedestal, the figure of Lincoln solemnly looks toward the Washington Monument, the Capitol, and beyond.

Since 1922 the Lincoln Memorial has been a ceremonial gathering place in times of national debate, protest, and celebration. Women struggling for equal rights gathered at the memorial, as did protesters against the Vietnam War. Martin Luther King, Jr., came here to demand civil rights for all races.

In 1865, immediately following Lincoln's death and long before the Lincoln Memorial was built, the grieving citizens of Washington raised funds for their own statue of Lincoln. The first public monument to the assassinated president was dedicated in 1869. Sculpted by a Washington gravestone carver, Lot Flannery, it was placed on a 35-foot-tall pedestal in front of the old City Hall. During the Lincoln Memorial's construction, however, this simple statue representing Lincoln as lawyer and

Abraham Lincoln statue
by Daniel Chester French, 1922.

The Emancipation Monument by Thomas Bell, 1876, Lincoln Park.

Lincoln statue by Lot Flannery, 1868, Judiciary Square.

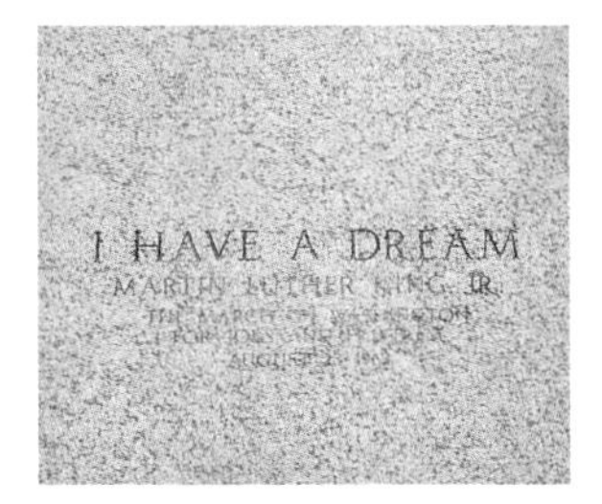

Inscription marking the location where Dr. Martin Luther King, Jr., gave his "I have a dream" speech on August 28, 1963.

statesman was placed in storage. Public outcry against its removal resulted in the statue's return to its original site, but without the tall pedestal.

In 1876 a second memorial to Lincoln, the Emancipation Monument, was erected in Lincoln Park on Capitol Hill. Charlotte Scott, a freed slave, made the first contribution to this memorial that was eventually paid for entirely by donations from emancipated slaves. Former slave and celebrated abolitionist Frederick Douglass offered the principal dedication speech, in which he stated: ". . . under [Lincoln's] wise and beneficent rule, we saw ourselves gradually lifted up from the depths of slavery to the heights of liberty and manhood."

Lincoln strongly believed in the experiment of popular government and in the triumph of right over wrong. His precise definition of democracy as "a government of the people, by the people, and for the people" is universally recognized and acclaimed. Lincoln was honest, hardworking, unprejudiced, farsighted, and witty. Once, when he was opposed unanimously by his cabinet secretaries, he drolly announced: "Seven nays, one aye; the ayes have it."

Mahatma Gandhi considered Lincoln to be "the greatest and noblest man of the nineteenth century"; Leo Tolstoy described him as "a humanitarian, as broad as the world"; and Secretary of War Edwin Stanton perceptively observed just after learning of Lincoln's death: "Now he belongs to the ages."

Franklin Delano Roosevelt Memorial

In 1941 Roosevelt was asked what sort of memorial he would prefer if one were to be built in his honor: ". . . I know exactly what I should like it to be. It should be a block about the size of this [his desk] and placed in the center of that green plot in front of the Archives Building. . . . plain, without ornamentation, with the simple carving 'In Memory of . . . '" In 1965 his request was honored.

Original FDR Memorial next to National Archives Building.

Franklin D. Roosevelt was an admired, trusted—and humble—leader. He transformed a nation in despair into a nation filled with hope during the Great Depression. Hence, in 1997, the last of Washington's twentieth-century memorials was dedicated to Roosevelt—this time more in proportion to the grandness of the man.

Neil Estern's seated statue of Roosevelt depicts him wearing the cape he wore to the Yalta Convention, with his favorite dog, Fala, seated next to him. The statue of his wife, Eleanor, is the only statue of a first lady to be honored at a presidential memorial. Waterfalls cascade down in each of the memorial's four parts, a nod to Roosevelt's fondness for water.

Both memorials, in their own way, represent this complex man who, with his aristocratic accent, exalted the "ordinary citizens," calling them his "fellow immigrants." His real memorial lies in the hearts and memories of those who understood Will Rogers' declaration: "Roosevelt swallowed our depression. He inhaled fear and exhaled confidence."

FDR with his Scottish terrier Fala, by Neil Estern, 1997.

President John F. Kennedy Gravesite

Monuments come in many forms. For President Kennedy there are two: one solemn and one joyous. Three days after the assassination of President Kennedy, his body was brought to Arlington Cemetery for burial. A low, circling granite wall was built surrounding his gravesite, inscribed with quotes from his inaugural address: "[T]he torch has been passed to a new generation of Americans. . . . Ask not what your country can do for you. Ask what you can do for your country. My fellow citizens of the world, ask not what America will do for you—but what together we can do for the freedom of man."

Jacqueline Kennedy requested that her husband's grave be marked with an eternal flame: a symbol ever since of the life and inspiration of one of America's most admired presidents. Melville Grosvenor, editor of the *National Geographic Magazine*, wrote of the flame: "[I]f we live to be a hundred, we will remember how he graced this earth and how he left it . . . but the deeds, the words, the examples of the man remain—and there will always be a flame to remind us."

John F. Kennedy's bust by Robert Barks, 1971, Grand Foyer of the Kennedy Center for the Performing Arts.

In 1971 a living memorial was dedicated to President Kennedy, reflecting a commitment to and enjoyment of the arts that he and the first lady brought to Washington: the Kennedy Center for the Performing Arts. An opera house, concert hall, the Eisenhower Theater, and two smaller theaters are housed in the Kennedy Center. More than 40 countries generously gave fabulous gifts, including crystal chandeliers, bronze statues, and modern tapestries to beautify the center in Kennedy's memory.

Artist Robert Berks sculpted the seven-foot-tall bronze bust of Kennedy that is centrally positioned in the center's tenth-of-a-mile-long grand foyer. Berks captured a twinkle in Kennedy's eye, a reminder of the wit of the president who once joked that Washington is a "city of northern charm and southern efficiency" and who self-effacingly introduced himself as "the man who accompanied Jacqueline Kennedy to Paris." He teased a gathering of Nobel Prize winners by saying that they were the most extraordinary collection of talent ever gathered at the White House, "with the possible exception of when Thomas Jefferson dined alone."

Kennedy looked beyond the present and called on his fellow Americans to reach beyond themselves. "I am certain," he said, "that after the dust of centuries has passed over our cities, we, too, will be remembered not for victories or defeats in battle or in politics, but for our contribution to the human spirit."

Theodore Roosevelt Island Park

Theodore Roosevelt is best remembered as the nation's first environmentalist president, the harbinger of sweeping changes in the American environmental conscience . . . and in the American landscape.

There could therefore be no more fitting memorial for Theodore Roosevelt than one that preserves and exalts the land. In 1932 an island in the Potomac River was renamed Theodore Roosevelt Island and a natural wildlife preserve was introduced. In 1967 a formal memorial to Roosevelt was added: a plaza surrounded by a moat and four tall, granite tablets inscribed with Roosevelt's eloquent philosophies. In the center of the plaza is artist Paul Manship's tall bronze statue of Roosevelt with one arm raised as if to begin his well-known speech: "There is delight in the hardy life of the open. There are no words that can tell the hidden spirit of the wilderness, that can reveal its mystery, its melancholy, and its charm."

Andrew Jackson Statue

Jackson was a man of firsts: the first president elected by the masses of common citizens, the first elected from the West, the first born in a log cabin, the first Democrat, and the first American honored with a bronze equestrian statue.

Dedicated on the thirty-eighth anniversary of the Battle of New Orleans, the Jackson statue depicts the general mounted proudly on his horse, glancing—and tipping his hat—toward the White House. Its sculptor, Clark Mills, admitted before taking the commission that he had never seen an equestrian statue, never seen Jackson, and had never cast anything in bronze . . . but he assured the Democratic Party that he could do it.

A stickler for details, Mills conducted his research most thoroughly: he purchased a horse, interviewed Jackson's friends, and borrowed everything of Jackson's that he could, from portraits to shoe buckles. Nearly eight years later, after considerable study, two different foundries, and eight different models, he was finally satisfied.

On January 8, 1853, a crowd of thousands came to cheer the unveiling of the perfectly balanced equestrian statue of General Jackson. So popular was Clark Mills' masterpiece that the state of Louisiana requested a second casting for New Orleans; a third casting is on display in Nashville.

Garfield Monument

President Hayes praised James Arthur Garfield with the words: "No man ever started so low that accomplished so much in all our history." Born in a log cabin on a farm in Ohio, Garfield worked hard to overcome every disadvantage of his childhood. Arriving in Washington already famous as a war hero of extraordinary bravery, he became a respected leader and popular orator as well during his 18 years at the Capitol. Upon reaching the pinnacle of his accomplishments, however, President Garfield's chance at glory was brought to an end just four months after his inauguration when he was assassinated at a Washington train station.

It was the Civil War veterans who had served under Garfield's command who spearheaded the movement to establish a memorial to their beloved lieutenant. John Quincy Adams Ward, a popular contemporary artist and acquaintance of Garfield, was chosen to sculpt a statue of the twentieth president.

In 1887 the memorial was unveiled: a bronze portrait statue depicting Garfield offering a speech, his inaugural address held in his left hand. Encircling the base are symbols of Garfield's life as scholar, soldier, and statesman: a young man studying a book, a warrior clutching his sword, and a toga-clad gentleman holding a tablet inscribed with the words "Law, Justice, Prosperity."

Sentinels of Freedom:
Our National Memorials

Arlington National Cemetery

"Arlington [is] where my affections and attachments are more strongly placed than any other place in the world," wrote Colonel Robert E. Lee in 1861. The 1,100-acre Arlington property belonged to Lee's father-in-law, George Washington Parke Custis, the adopted son of George and Martha Washington.

For 30 years Lee and his family lived at Arlington. On April 19, 1861, their lives changed irreversibly when Lee, a lifelong military officer, was offered command of the newly formed Union army of the Potomac. Lee owned no slaves, he disliked the institution of slavery, and he supported the preservation of the Union. However, he also opposed the abolitionist movement and his loyalty was to his home state of Virginia—which had just seceded.

In an agonizing decision, Lee resigned from the U.S. Army and accepted the command of Virginia's militia. He moved his family to Richmond; Arlington was seized by the Union army for the defense of Washington and was later auctioned to the government for non-payment of taxes. In 1864 Union General M. C. Meigs spitefully recommended that the land surrounding Arlington House should become a national cemetery; the first burials took place immediately.

After the deaths of Mary Anna and Robert E. Lee in the 1870s, their oldest son took legal action to regain his inheritance of the Arlington property. When a Virginia court ruled in his favor, the federal government appealed the case to the Supreme Court, but lost. The Lee family accepted $150,000 in payment from the government for the land that had become the cemetery. At their request, however, the house was returned to the Lees; they restored and opened it to the public, but eventually transferred it to the care of the National Park Service. Of the original 1,100 acres of land, 612 are used for burials, with as many as 25 new burials a day; the balance of the land belongs to Fort Myer, home of the Old Guard.

On November 11, 1921, Americans paid tribute to all who perished in World War I, especially those who did not return, by entombing the body of an unknown soldier at Arlington Cemetery. A military honor guard was established at the tomb, made up of select members of the Third U.S. Army Infantry Regiment, known as the Old Guard. The tomb is guarded day and night, and a changing-of-the-guard ceremony is carried out on a scheduled basis.

Three more tombs were dedicated to honor those soldiers still missing from World War II and

Morning Room, Arlington House, Robert E. Lee Memorial.

Previous spread: View from Arlington National Cemetery.

the conflicts in Korea and Vietnam. On the large marble sarcophagus over the tomb of the World War I unknown soldier are carved three figures representing Peace, Victory, and Valor, along with the solemn phrase: "Here Rests in Honored Glory an American Soldier Known but to God."

On the hill in front of Arlington House, Washington's city planner, Pierre L'Enfant, was reburied in 1909. In his own time, L'Enfant's genius was not acknowledged: he lived much of his life by the charity of others, died in Maryland in abject poverty, and was buried in a poorly marked grave. Eighty years after his death, L'Enfant's remains were found and reinterred at the site overlooking the capital city he had envisioned 120 years earlier. At the gravesite's dedication, a Latin phrase was borrowed from Sir Christopher Wren's tomb in London's St. Paul's Cathedral, a church that Wren had designed: *si monumentum requiris, circumspice*—("if a monument is required, look around").

Pierre L'Enfant tomb.

The Tomb of the Unknown Soldier.

HERE RESTS IN
HONORED GLORY
AN AMERICA
SOLDIER
NOWN BUT TO GO

World War II Memorial

As Tom Brokaw wrote about America's World War II generation: "They answered the call to save the world from . . . fascist maniacs. They faced great odds . . . but they did not protest. They succeeded on every front. They won the war." The World War II Memorial commemorates their sacrifice and celebrates their victory

World War II was the largest, most catastrophic event in human history; it defined the twentieth century. The memorial to honor that struggle of free men and women against totalitarianism was a long time in the making. Less than one-quarter of those who served in the military were alive when the memorial was dedicated on May 31, 2004, but more than 200,000 veterans and family members came to Washington for the celebration. They came not for glory but as a tribute to those who could not come.

FDR quote with Washington Monument.

The memorial was carefully placed between the Washington Monument and the Lincoln Memorial, references to the cardinal moments in our history in each of the preceding centuries. Just as George Washington was the father of our freedoms and Abraham Lincoln preserved and extended them; the World War II generation perpetuated those freedoms for future generations.

Two grand arched entrance pavilions, inscribed with the words *Atlantic* and *Pacific*, stand for the foremost theaters of the two-front war. Each pavilion has four columns—one each for the Army, Navy, Air Force, and Marines. Fifty-six pillars encircle the 7.4-acre site, representing the 48 states and 8 territories of the United States during the war years. The columns are connected by a bronze rope symbolizing the nation's unity of purpose. Wreaths of wheat stalks and of oak leaves decorate the state columns, signifying the agricultural and industrial strength of the country.

Centered in the grand open plaza are the Rainbow Pool and Fountains, making a joyous, celebratory statement. To the west, two formal waterfalls frame the solemn Field of Stars with more than 4,000 individual stars, each representing 100 Americans who died in World War II. During the war, families placed blue stars in the windows of their homes—one star for every family member on active duty. Each gold star symbolized a death.

At the memorial's dedication, former president George H. W. Bush commented, "These were average men and women who lived in extraordinary times." One 78-year-old memorial visitor explained, "You appreciated life. You learned how fragile it was. You grew up in a hurry." Another visitor, a veteran, simply said, "There was nothing else you could do but do your best."

"America will never forget their sacrifices."
—Harry S Truman

Field of Stars.

Detail of the Memorial Plaza.

PACIFIC

Vietnam Veterans Memorial

The Vietnam Veterans Memorial has been called "[t]he greatest aesthetic achievement in an American public monument in the twentieth century." Building a memorial in memory of those who lost their lives in the Vietnam War was the idea of veteran Jan Scruggs. He enlisted help from other veterans, raised funds, located a site, and planned a competition for the memorial's design. It was not to be a political place but one for contemplation, harmonious with its surroundings, where the names of all the missing and dead are remembered.

It was "the power of a name"—the names of the more than 50,000 soldiers who died in the Vietnam War—that inspired Maya Lin as she prepared a memorial design; her vision, on the other hand, she felt was guided by a need to be "honest about the reality of war, about the loss of life in war, about remembering those who served and especially those who had died." In the end, she chose to acknowledge the lives without focusing on the war.

The memorial was dedicated in 1982 just as Maya Lin designed it, but only after tremendous controversy nearly succeeded in canceling the plans. Placed into a chevron-shaped cut in the earth, the ends of each row of the polished, mirror-like granite tablets etched with names point toward the Lincoln Memorial and the Washington Monument. The names are chronologically listed by date of death, beginning at the tallest panel of the east wall and ending with the tallest panel of the west wall, a

design that places together the names of those who fought and died together.

Two years later Frederick Hart's sculpted statue of three soldiers was placed at a distance from the memorial; they seem to stare at—and beyond—the names etched on the memorial wall. Glenna Goodacre's sculpture of three nurses and a dying soldier was dedicated nearby to the women who served at home and abroad during the Vietnam War.

The Vietnam Veterans Memorial continues to evoke heartfelt emotions from visitors who pause to touch one of the 58,235 names, to leave a memento to a loved one who is honored there . . . or simply to not forget.

Korean War Veterans Memorial

"Determination combined with fear . . . what a soldier experiences in battle." With this thought in mind, artist Frank Gaylord captured an astonishing expressiveness on the portrait-like faces of 19 statues of soldiers, frozen in time at the Korean War Veterans Memorial.

The cool, gray, unpolished stainless-steel statues are reflected in the tall black granite wall beside them. The reflection doubles the number of 19 soldiers to an illusory 38, representative of the 38th parallel—the boundary between North and South Korea. The solemn statues are compelling in their postures, gestures, and glances, all of which reveal their fatigue and anxiety. They seem to cautiously move toward a goal, toward their symbol of freedom: the waving American flag on a tall pole in front of and high above them.

Etched on the wall are 2,500 shadowy faces of those who served in support of the troops during the Korean War, including the supply clerks, mechanics, crew chiefs, cooks, nurses, and chaplains. These images seem to float in front of the reflection of the ghostly statues of foot-soldiers in combat dress and foul-weather, windblown ponchos. "They are anonymous, thereby rendering a universal portrait," explained one of the designers, Louis Nelson.

The Korean War was the first conflict fought as a United Nations operation, and the memorial honors all of the U.N. troops that served. In June of 1950, North Korean troops crossed the 38th parallel into South Korea, claiming a nationalist mandate to reunify the divided country. The United Nations Security Council voted to send troops to recapture Seoul and to counter the invasion. Twenty countries sent troops to serve in Korea, but 90 percent of the non-Korean, U.N. troops were American. By July 27, 1953, when the combat ceased, more than 33,600 Americans had been killed in action (2,700 of whom died in captivity), 8,000 Americans were missing in action, and 103,000 had been wounded.

"Freedom is not free" is the one phrase inscribed on the memorial wall: a simple expression that brings home the reality of dedication to duty and patriotism and of the willingness to sacrifice for the cause of freedom. In its quiet dignity, the memorial resounds with the gratitude of America for all soldiers of all wars.

United States Marine Corps War Memorial

(The Iwo Jima Memorial)

The most ferocious battle of World War II was the struggle for a tiny island in the Pacific, a Japanese stronghold called Iwo Jima. "Fear was a friend in a time like that. It made you wary, careful," explained former marine Thomas Miller, a participant in what became the greatest amphibious assault in history.

Iwo Jima means Sulfur Island; actually, the island is an inactive volcano 7.5 square miles in size and 650 miles south of Tokyo, which by 1945 concealed 22,000 Japanese troops in the 16 miles of underground tunnels they had dug. For 36 days Americans fought against an unseen but highly organized enemy. In the end, nearly 7,000 Americans died (87 percent of whom were marines) and 21,900 were wounded.

On the fourth day of the month-long battle, an American flag was carried by the Marines to the top of the island's highest peak, Mount Suribachi, and raised up on a pole for all to see. This was the first American flag to fly over Japanese enemy territory, and it was reported that soldiers shouted and wept, that ships' whistles blew and their bells rang out to celebrate the taking of Mount Suribachi.

Later in the day, when a second, much larger flag was taken to Suribachi to replace the first one, newsman Joe Rosenthal photographed it being raised. Six soldiers struggled together against strong mountain-top winds to hoist up the huge 4½-by-8-foot American flag attached to a pipe weighing 150 pounds. The photograph, which was featured on the front page of newspapers around the world, won a Pulitzer Prize for Rosenthal and has become an American icon.

Of the six men represented in the statue, three died on Iwo Jima: 25-year-old unit leader Sgt. Mike Strank, nicknamed "the old man"; 20-year-old Cpl. Harlon Block of Texas; and 19-year-old Pfc. Franklin Sousley of Kentucky. The three survivors were: 22-year-old Cpl. Ira Hayes, a Pima Indian from Arizona who only lived to be 33; 19-year-old Pfc. Rene Gagnon of New Hampshire, who died in 1979; and 21-year-old Pharmacist Mate John Bradley from Wisconsin, who lived until 1994 but rarely spoke of his role in the flag-raising at Iwo Jima.

Navy combat artist Felix de Weldon was so inspired by the patriotic picture from Iwo Jima when he saw it in the newspaper that he sculpted a small, illustrative wax model of it. After World War II, de Weldon was commissioned to create the memorial for the Marines; using Rosenthal's photograph, he sculpted a statue about five times the actual size of the six flag raisers on Mount Suribachi.

The U.S. Marine Corps War Memorial, also called the Iwo Jima Memorial, honors all marines who have served and died in the struggle for freedom since the U.S. Marine Corps was founded on November 10, 1775. Etched and gilded on the memorial wall are the words of Admiral Chester Nimitz describing the courage and determination of the U.S. Marines: "Uncommon Valor Was a Common Virtue."

BOXER·REBELLION·1900 × NICARAGUA·1912 × VERA·CRUZ·1914 × HAITI·1915-1934 × SANTO·DOMINGO·1916-1924 × WORLD·WAR·I·1917-1918
PERSIAN·GULF·1987-1991 × PANAMA·1988-1990
IN HONOR AND MEMORY
OF THE MEN OF THE
UNITED STATES MARINE CORPS
WHO HAVE GIVEN
THEIR LIVES TO THEIR COUNTRY

National Law Enforcement Officers Memorial

"It is not how these officers died that made them heroes, it is how they lived," wrote Vivian Eney, whose husband, Sergeant Christopher S. Eney, was the first U.S. Capitol policeman to die in the line of duty. Her words are inscribed on one of the low entry walls of the National Law Enforcement Officers Memorial.

Since 1792 more than 16,000 peacekeeping officers have lost their lives performing their duty, somber statistics that serve as a reminder of the dangers that law enforcement officers face every day. Two hundred years after the first recorded federal officer's death, this memorial was dedicated.

A geometrical, interlacing pattern of pavement on the memorial's oval-shaped plaza leads to the bronze medallion in the center. Embossed on the medallion are a shield and a rose: the shield is the universally recognized symbol of law enforcement, and the rose is symbolic of remembrance and the love of a grateful nation. The central plaza is surrounded with double rows of linden trees and thousands of daffodils that burst into bloom in early spring, followed in mid-May by hundreds of brilliant azaleas.

Two concave, mirror-image marble walls encircle the plaza and form two "paths of remembrance." On the upper portions these low memorial walls are randomly inscribed with the names of the thousands of federal, state, and local law enforcement officers killed in the line of duty. Even more compelling, however, is the large blank space below those names, waiting to be filled. Sadly, several hundred names are added each year.

At the ends of the memorial walls are symbolic statues of lions and lionesses watching over sleeping cubs that seem oblivious to danger. The lions are alert and in an aggressive posture, ready to defend against evil. The lionesses are in peaceful repose, one paw draped over the wall, vigilantly guarding the innocent cubs. Inscribed on an entry wall beneath one of the lion statues is a fitting biblical reference: "The wicked flee when no man pursueth: but the righteous are as bold as a lion" (Proverbs 28:1).

African-American Civil War Memorial

"Black soldiers had a real love of country . . . a love of the land and a desire to prove their manhood and be compensated with winning their right to freedom," explained American University Professor Ed Smith. African-Americans were first allowed to join the military in 1863, and by the end of the Civil War they made up 10 percent of the Union Army.

The African American Civil War Memorial was established 130 years after the Civil War ended, in recognition of the role played by African Americans—both freedmen and slaves—who volunteered for service during the Civil War. The memorial honors more than 178,000 black Union soldiers and their 7,000 white officers who served together in 166 U.S. colored troop regiments.

"The Spirit of Freedom" is the name that artist Ed Hamilton gave to the 9½-foot-tall, bronze, semi-circular sculpture he designed. On the front of the sculpture are three infantrymen and one sailor, standing tall as fighters for freedom. On the rear are statues representing their families: father, mother, grandmother, and children, acknowledging the men with great emotion as they go off to war. To symbolize the spiritual nature of the piece, Hamilton added a protective figure floating above the soldiers and sailor.

United States Air Force Memorial

"It is just an unbelievable feeling of soaring into the heavens when you look at it," said retired Air Force Maj. Gen. Edward F. Grillo, as he described the three gracefully arching stainless steel spires of United States Air Force Memorial.

The late James Ingo Freed, the memorial's architect, said his inspiration came from watching television film footage of a team of Air Force jets shooting skyward in unison, creating high-rising vapor trails that curl over at their tops. The Air Force calls this "the bomb burst" maneuver. Although these gleaming spires appear almost weightless, they are made of 17,000 tons of steel and concrete. Their heights vary from 210 to 270 feet and their velvety metallic finish is reminiscent of aircraft skin.

The memorial honors those who served in the Air Force and its predecessor services, dating back to the U.S. Army Air Corps of the early 1900s. The memorial site overlooks Arlington Cemetery, as well as the northwest wall of the Pentagon that was hit by American Airlines Flight 77 on September 11, 2001. This precipice has served as a place of contemplation ever since that tragic day. The panoramic view from this high promontory brings into focus Washington's familiar landmarks and offers the viewer a bird's-eye perspective of the city.

© Samuel Jolly

First Division Monument

The First Division had "a special pride of service and a high state of morale never broken by hardship nor battle," said General J. J. Pershing of the division that became known as "Pershing's Own." This oldest division of the U.S. Army traces its roots back to colonial times. During World War I its members were the first American troops to arrive in Europe and the last to leave, losing 5,516 men in between. After the war, a proposal was made to commemorate the division's extraordinary sacrifice. A prominent site south of the War Department Building was selected and architect Cass Gilbert's 35-foot-tall, pink polished-granite column was erected. Around the granite base are inscribed the names of the First Division's casualties. An 18-foot-tall gilded bronze statue of winged Victory watches over the memorial from atop the column. Artist Daniel Chester French placed her standing precariously on a globe, grasping a flag in her right hand and extending her left in a gesture of benediction to those named below. Later additions honor the thousands of First Infantry Division soldiers who perished in World War II, the Vietnam War, and Operation Desert Storm.

Second Division Memorial

"SECOND TO NONE" is the motto of the Second Infantry Division of the U.S. Army, which was founded with America's entry into World War I. Originally the Second Division was composed of one brigade each of infantry, marines, and artillery, along with various supporting units. In memory of the thousands of soldiers killed in France during World War I, President Franklin D. Roosevelt dedicated a memorial "symbolizing the splendid achievements of the Second Division" just south of the White House.

John Russell Pope, the memorial's architect, designed a huge pink-granite portal flanked by two slightly lower walls. The walls are decorated with carved laurel wreathes and inscribed with the gilded names of the battles in which the division participated. The memorial was later extended to include two wings: one honoring the fallen of World War II, the other commemorating those who perished in the Korean War. Artist James Earle Fraser sculpted a giant, fiery, gilded sword that blocks the portal—a symbolic impediment against the German advance on Paris.

United States Navy Memorial

"Any man who may be asked . . . what he did to make his life worthwhile . . . can respond with a good deal of pride and satisfaction, 'I served in the United States Navy.'" These words of President Kennedy are inscribed on the steps of the United States Navy Memorial Plaza. The first suggestion to erect a navy memorial in Washington came from the city's planner, L'Enfant, but two centuries passed before the idea was realized.

The Navy Memorial's central plaza displays the world's largest map, 100 feet in diameter, illustrating the vastness of the world's oceans. A statue by Stanley Bleifeld of a classic American sailor, the collar of his peacoat turned up and his hand thrust into his pockets, stands alone in the plaza; he appears confident, vigilant, and, perhaps, longing for home.

Encircling the plaza are 26 bronze relief panels with scenes commemorating events in naval history and honoring communities of naval service. Two fountain pools of cascading water, salted with water from the seven seas and the Great Lakes, encircle the southern hemisphere of the plaza. The east pool honors U.S. Navy servicemen and –women. The west pools honors international navies and is inscribed with this quote of solidarity: "To shipmates from other lands the waters that divide us unite us."

Pentagon Memorial

©T.J. Kirkpatrick/Corbis

"We claim this ground in remembrance of the events of September 11, 2001, to honor the 184 people whose lives were lost, their families, and all who sacrifice that we may live in freedom. We will never forget."

These words are inscribed on the entry stone of the Pentagon Memorial, the first national 9/11 memorial. A small, determined group of victims' family members raised the funds and held the design competition, insisting that the memorial should rise on the grounds of the building's west side, exactly where the plane hit.

Keith Kaseman and Julie Beckman, a young couple barely out of graduate school, submitted the winning design, which filled the two-acre space with shade trees interspersed among rows of arcing, cantilevered "light" steel benches. The benches rise up from the ground as if taking flight. Each is mirrored in a rectangular pool of trickling water that contains an underwater light to shine on the bench's underside at night, setting the entire site aglow.

The benches are oriented along the trajectory of American Airlines Flight 77. Each has a nameplate and is placed in a time-line representing the ages of the victims: from 3-year old Dana Falkenberg, to John Yamnicky, 71. The benches are arranged according to whether victims were killed on the plane or in the building. If, when reading a name, the Pentagon is in the background that person died in the building; if the sky is the background, the person died on the plane.

WISDOM LINGERS
WISDOM IS THE PRINCIPAL
THEREFORE GET WISDOM AND
THY GETTING GET

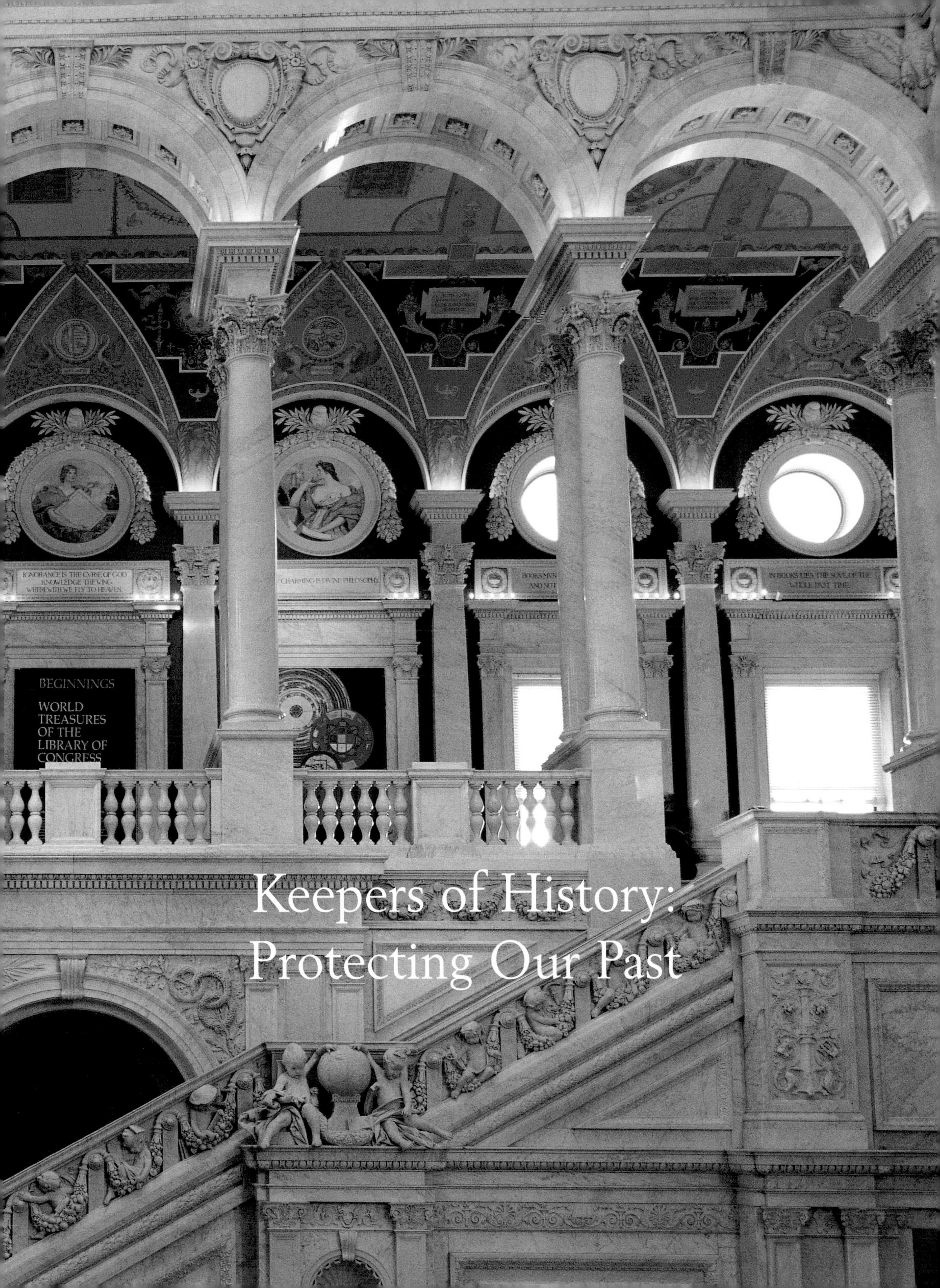

Keepers of History: Protecting Our Past

National Archives Building

"I have long thought that the best way to make the American people acquainted with the history of their country is to render accessible to them the sources of that history," wrote James Parton in 1858. Three-quarters of a century later, the National Archives was established as an independent agency, created to maintain and preserve the records of the nation and to make these resources available to everyone.

The National Archives and Records Administration (NARA) is nicknamed "the nation's memory" because its function is to filter through the records of the country's official life and decide what is worth saving. Actually, a very small percentage of the government's paperwork is considered to have lasting value to the nation or to individual citizens.

Among the preserved items are billions of pages of text; millions of maps, charts, and photographs; and hundreds of thousands of historical sound recordings and reels of movie film. Major archival holdings date from 1775 and include the Louisiana Purchase Treaty, the Emancipation Proclamation, and the deed to the gift of the Statue of Liberty. The general records include census schedules, military service and pension records, diaries, and family Bibles.

Previous page:
Library of Congress.

The most important documents in the National Archives are the ones on permanent display: the Charters of Freedom. The Declaration of Independence has changed history through the power of its words and ideas on the universality of human rights. The U.S. Constitution—the most enduring written constitution in the world—defined a new type of government that promotes the welfare of all its citizens. The Bill of Rights provides for revisions and changes to the Constitution; these first Ten Amendments grant individuals the freedoms of speech, press, religion, and assembly.

"Study the past," advised Confucius, whose quote is one of many carved on the exterior of the National Archives Building. "Eternal vigilance is the price of Liberty," warns Thomas Jefferson in another of the building's inscriptions. And a quote from Shakespeare cleverly observes, "What is past is prologue."

Rotunda for the Charters of Freedom, shown from left to right: The Declaration of Independence, all four pages of the United States Constitution, and the Bill of Rights. Courtesy of NARA.

Library of Congress

"There is no subject to which a Member of Congress may not have occasion to refer," said Thomas Jefferson of the Congressional Library's collection. After a fire set by the British in 1814 destroyed the Capitol's original collection of 3,000 books, Jefferson convinced Congress, despite many strong objections, to purchase 6,700 volumes from his own personal library, including works in seven languages on a multitude of subjects.

A second disastrous fire in 1851 destroyed 35,000 volumes, two-thirds of the library's collection. Thirteen years later Ainsworth Spofford was appointed librarian and promised to bring Congress "oceans of books and rivers of information, free." Spofford's greatest contribution was the fulfillment of his promise through the centralization of all copyright activity within the library. Under the new copyright law, two copies of all registered items had to be deposited in the library—free of charge to the library, of course. An international copyright law likewise increased the library's collection of foreign works.

By the early 1870s the library's fast-growing collection, still housed in the Capitol, had outgrown its allotted space and the construction of a new library building became necessary. Beginning in 1889, the Army Corps of Engineers worked together with 50 American artists for eight years to create one of the most magnificent government-owned structures in the country. The library's inspiring frescoes, mosaics, and murals in marble, granite, and bronze celebrate the achievements of Western civilization.

Serving as the research branch of Congress, the library is dedicated to accumulating everything ever known by all civilizations. It is the largest international library in the world, with more than 126 million items in 450 languages, stored on 535 miles of shelves in three buildings named for three influential presidents: Jefferson, Adams, and Madison. Approximately 7,000 new items are added each day to the library's collection, which includes books, pamphlets, newspapers, documents, manuscripts, maps, atlantes, artwork, prints, photographs, sound recordings, films, and the largest comic book collection in the world.

Thomas Jefferson understood that the power of the intellect could—and must—shape a free and democratic society. The Library of Congress is one of Jefferson's greatest legacies to the nation, the embodiment of his faith in learning and his belief that self-government can only work through the unhampered pursuit of truth.

THE INQVIRY, KNOWLEDGE, AND BELIEF OF TRVTH IS THE SOVEREIGN GOOD OF HVMAN NATVRE.
AS ONE LAMP LIGHTS ANOTHER NOR GROWS LESS SO NOBLENESS ENKINDLETH NOBLENESS.
ART

Smithsonian

THE CASTLE

In 1838 a prominent English chemist and respected mineralogist left an amazing fortune—105 bags of gold sovereigns valued at $508,318—to a country he had never visited. "The property is bequeathed," declares James Smithson's will, "to the United States of America to found at Washington . . . the Smithsonian Institution."

After receiving notification of Smithson's gift, members of Congress hotly debated the constitutionality of accepting such a generous bequest. Finally, at the urging of John Quincy Adams, Congress accepted the benefaction in 1846 and created the Smithsonian Institution. Nine years later the first building was erected and named "the Castle." The multi-purpose structure designed by James Renwick became the symbol of the Smithsonian Institution.

From the very beginning the Castle was employed, in accordance with Mr. Smithson's will, as "an establishment for the increase and diffusion of knowledge among men." Modern scientific laboratories were installed and the top scientists of the day were invited to come pursue their research there. The first weather reports were transmitted from one of the Castle's towers using Morse's new invention, the telegraph. And during the Civil War, President Lincoln came to watch the balloonist Thaddeus S. C. Lowe demonstrate his ideas on employing hot-air balloons for military observation purposes.

The Smithsonian Institution is the largest museum complex in the world, comprising 18 museum buildings and the National Zoo, and housing a collection of 145 million items, to which 1.6 million are added each year. Nicknamed "the Nation's Attic," the Smithsonian refuses to part with any acquisition on the grounds that it is impossible to know what might be of interest and value to future generations.

"To furnish the means of acquiring knowledge is the greatest benefit that can be conferred upon mankind. It prolongs life itself, and enlarges the sphere of existence," wrote John Quincy Adams in defense of Smithson's bequest, ". . . it is no extravagance of anticipation to declare that [Smithson's] name will be hereafter enrolled among the eminent benefactors of mankind."

Smithsonian

NATIONAL MUSEUM OF AMERICAN HISTORY

"I hope every schoolchild who visits this capital, every foreign visitor who comes to this First City, and every doubter who hesitates before the onrush of tomorrow will someday spend some time in this great museum," said President Lyndon Johnson at the 1964 dedication of the National Museum of History and Technology, renamed the National Museum of American History in 1980.

In the late nineteenth century, the Smithsonian Institution agreed to establish a national museum that would include a separate division to document the history of technology, invention, and engineering. Under its auspices, an accumulation of objects related to American history—such as those transferred from the National Cabinet of Curiosities at the Patent Office and the exhibits from the 1876 Centennial Exposition in Philadelphia—could finally be suitably cared for at the Smithsonian.

Opposite page: The flag unfurled at the Pentagon on September 12, 2001. The banner, a garrison flag, draped the damaged west wall of the Pentagon for nearly a month.

Throughout the first half of the twentieth century, hundreds of thousands of books, pamphlets, product catalogues, trade journals, and other miscellaneous items all related to engineering, technology, and history, were given to the Smithsonian Institution. By the 1950s the institution was in desperate need of a separate building in which to properly safeguard and display the collection.

The National Museum of American History has become one of the most visited and best-loved of the Smithsonian museums. On exhibit is a vast assemblage of Americana, including the original Star-Spangled Banner, some of the first ladies' gowns, presidential campaign memorabilia, Judy Garland's red slippers from *The Wizard of Oz*, the Lone Ranger's black mask, a 1937 Electrolux vacuum cleaner, the original "Bakelizer" used to make the world's first plastic, the Revolutionary War gunboat *Philadelphia*, rare musical instruments, the Ring King Krispy Kreme doughnut machine, a 1957 Chevy automobile, and Horatio Greenough's godlike statue of George Washington. Everything in the collection has a unique story to tell and, as the guardian of all "things" American, the museum offers the world a truly American experience.

Smithsonian

NATIONAL MUSEUM OF NATURAL HISTORY

From 1838 to 1842 Admiral Charles Wilkes amassed mountains of natural treasures on a daring, around-the-world discovery voyage. For 15 years after he brought them home to Washington, Wilkes carefully catalogued his 4,000 zoological specimens, 50,000 plants, and 2,500 artifacts. The enormous collection was then transferred to the newly established Smithsonian Institution for safekeeping.

Storage space in the Smithsonian Castle soon proved insufficient and, by 1881, a new national museum was built. The collection continued to increase so rapidly that a second national museum had to be opened in 1910, which was named the Natural History Museum. Its main purpose was to collect, preserve, study, and display specimens from the natural world and objects made by its inhabitants in order to reveal the history of the planet, life, and the diversity of humankind and nature.

The pink fairy armadillo and a rare African okapi are among the hundreds of animals in the new Hall of Mammals. The most memorable mammal, however, is Henry, "the greatest elephant of all." In 1959 this noble African bush elephant was placed on exhibit in the center of the museum's great rotunda. While alive, Henry weighed 8 tons, stood 13 feet and 2 inches tall at the withers, and carried tusks that were 7 feet long. His skin was so heavy that 23 attendants were necessary just to carry it, and taxidermists took 16 months to create a model on which to mount it.

More than 120 million items are stored in the museum's repository, including fossils, minerals, meteorites, stuffed mammals, bones, the jaws of a prehistoric shark, and an 80-foot-long dinosaur specimen from Utah. Reptiles displayed in the herpetology exhibits include Komodo dragons, iguanas, and a king cobra. Live insects are in the Insect Zoo: scorpions, katydids, beetles, tarantulas, and Madagascar hissing cockroaches—some of which may be petted.

By far the most popular item in the Minerals and Gems Collection is the 45.52-carat, blue Hope Diamond, on display with the 38-carat Chalk Emerald and the 423-carat Logan Sapphire. The Hope Diamond is named for its nineteenth-century owner, British banker Henry T. Hope. Washington socialite Evalyn Walsh McLean purchased the Hope in 1910 and set it in a platinum frame featuring 16 diamonds, suspended from a platinum chain with 46 diamonds. She then dangled the 91-carat, pear-shaped Star of the East diamond beneath it. After Evalyn McLean's death, jeweler Harry Winston purchased the Hope at an auction and donated it to the Smithsonian Institution. Realizing the difficulty of insuring and transporting such a priceless object, Winston simply sent it to Washington via the postal service, wrapped in brown paper and packaged in a small box.

Pages 83–84: African bush elephant in the newly renovated Rotunda at the Smithsonian National Museum of Natural History. Photo by Chip Clark ©Smithsonian Institution.

IMAX
Bugs!
in 3D
NOW SHOWING
IMAX
T-REX
BACK TO THE CRETACEOUS
NOW IN IMAX 3D!
NOW SHOWING
AFRICAN VOICES
Hall of African History and Culture
"Look back and Remember"
Smithsonian
National Museum of Natural History

AINU

1st FLOOR
DIRECTORY

National Geographic Society

"The eye must see before the mind can believe," said Gilbert H. Grosvenor, editor of the *National Geographic Magazine*. In 1915 Grosvenor laid down the seven principles which still guide the society: (1) absolute accuracy; (2) an abundance of instructive and artistic illustrations; (3) everything printed must have permanent value; (4) notes of a trivial character are avoided; (5) nothing of a partisan or controversial nature is printed; (6) only what is of a kindly nature is printed about any country or people; (7) the content is planned with a view of being timely.

Once considered a technical journal of scientific lectures, the society's magazine became a popular, attractive monthly written for the layman. Grosvenor was a pioneer in the use of photo illustration and featured articles that were written by congressmen and presidents. Originally membership was only by invitation, but by 1926 membership had reached one million.

The society's first headquarters were located a few blocks north of the White House. In 1964 the society constructed the most striking and modern office building in Washington and opened the ground-floor Explorer's Hall to the public. In 1985 the society's third edifice, a terraced building with a garden-like plaza, was completed.

"Why not popularize the science of geography and take it into the homes of the people?" asked Alexander Graham Bell, first president of the society and father-in-law to Grosvenor, in 1899. "Why not transform the society's magazine into a vehicle for carrying the living, breathing, human-interest truth about this great world of ours?" More than a century later, the National Geographic Society has done all that and more.

Smithsonian

NATIONAL MUSEUM OF THE AMERICAN INDIAN

"You absolutely have to tell the truth in this museum . . . the true history of Native people." Repeated by many Native Americans, this request became the mandate for the design of the National Museum of the American Indian, the first national museum dedicated to the history and cultures of the indigenous people of the Americas.

The museum was constructed primarily to house the abundant treasures of George Gustav Heye (pronounced "high"), who spent 49 years assembling the most comprehensive collection of Native American art and artifacts in the world: 800,000 objects from more than 1,000 tribes, spanning 10,000 years and including Chief Geronimo's hat and Sitting Bull's drum.

The New York businessman made his first fateful purchase in 1897, an act that led him to "acquire other objects as opportunity offered." Heye's obsession earned him a reputation as a "great vacuum cleaner of a collector," and as a "boxcar collector," when he began shipping the discoveries of anthropological expeditions—which he financed—to himself in railway boxcars. Never mind his quirky collecting habits, though: Heye single-handedly rescued an irreplaceable living record of American indigenous culture.

The Minnesota Kasota-stone facade of the museum building was designed to evoke images of natural cliffs weathered by wind and water. One group of Native American men from a matriarchal tribe perceived the swirling, curving building as hospitable and nurturing: "We really want to congratulate you on designing the first female building on the National Mall."

Smithsonian

NATIONAL AIR AND SPACE MUSEUM

On July 4, 1976, President Gerald Ford proclaimed the newly dedicated National Air and Space Museum "America's birthday gift to itself." In the first month it was open, more than one million visitors came to see this museum that seemed to embody the American spirit of adventure.

President Lincoln and Joseph Henry, the first secretary of the Smithsonian, shared an interest in aeronautics: both experimented with the use of hot-air balloons for military purposes. Fifty years later the combined efforts of the Smithsonian Institution and Alexander Graham Bell persuaded Congress to establish the National Advisory Committee for Aeronautics, the forerunner of NASA (the National Aeronautics and Space Administration). By 1920 the Smithsonian displayed a few aeronautical exhibits; as technology grew, however, so did the collection, and in 1946 the National Air Museum, as it was originally called, was chartered.

Thirty years later the history of aviation was more fully presented in a new, specially designed museum building filled with popular displays: early warplanes, passenger planes, a moon rock, the lunar-lander, and Spacelab. Also on display are the Wright Brothers' canvas and wood flyer; Charles Lindbergh's tiny Spirit of St. Louis, which drastically expanded the scope of flight and transformed the 25-year-old pilot into America's first media superstar; and the *Apollo 11* space module that brought astronauts back to America from the first visit to the moon and carried America into a new age of discovery. All of the exhibits underscore the idea that twentieth-century technology has been defined by the airplane.

The museum's collection of aviation materials is the largest in the world, but until recently

The 1903 Wright Flyer.

80 percent of it has been held in storage. On the one hundredth anniversary of the Wright Brothers' first flight, the Smithsonian's new Udvar-Hazy Center opened in a facility near Washington-Dulles Airport. More than 200 aircraft and hundreds of aviation artifacts are on exhibit, including the space shuttle *Enterprise*, the world's fastest jet named the Blackbird, the B-29 Superfortress *Enola Gay* that dropped the atomic bomb on Hiroshima, and the world's only supersonic passenger airliner, the Concorde. "Almost everything we have today in terms of comfort has come from air and space research," explained museum director John R. Dailey. "Flight is the crowning achievement of our century."

USAF
IMAX
SPACE STATION 3D
NOW SHOWING

National Building Museum

(The Old Pension Building)

The Great Hall of the National Building Museum, located in what was once the Old Pension Building, was described by architect Philip Johnson as "the most astonishing interior space in America." Larger than a football field, the hall is covered by a roof two acres in size and supported by the world's highest Corinthian-style columns.

Built as a modern office building in the 1880s, the Old Pension Building was filled with natural light and fresh circulating air, an architectural wonder that provided undreamed-of comfort for government workers. General Montgomery C. Meigs designed the building large enough to accommodate the 1,500 clerks who dispensed Civil War pension benefits to veterans and their families. It was also intended that the Great Hall be used for national ceremonies, and six inaugural balls, from Grover Cleveland to William Howard Taft, were held there.

Meigs modeled the building after the Palazzo Farnese in Rome, but he doubled the size and used 15.5 million bricks in its construction, thereby creating the largest brick structure in the world—and a fireproof building in fire-plagued Washington. He engineered such innovations as dumbwaiters and conveyors to facilitate the movement of documents and designed stairways with deep treads and low risers to make the climb easier for elderly or disabled veterans. Encircling the building's exterior is a quarter-mile-long, decorative, sculpted frieze of Union soldiers and sailors, eternally marching, rowing, and riding on horseback. The building itself was a memorial to the veterans of the Civil War, and between 1879 and 1924, $5.7 trillion in pensions was distributed at the Pension Building to those veterans and their dependents.

In 1968 the first suggestion was made to transform the Old Pension Building into a museum dedicated to the building arts. Ten years later a proposal was presented to Congress, and in 1985 the first galleries were opened in the new museum that celebrates great and small accomplishments in American building and design. Inaugural balls are also once again held in the Great Hall. Proclaimed the *Washington Post*'s architectural critic, Benjamin Forgey: "Of all the arts and trades, none affects the lives of more people than architecture and building, and of all the structures in Washington, none suits the teaching of these subjects better than the Pension Building."

United States Holocaust Memorial Museum

"Most museums deal in the beautiful—we deal in the anti-beautiful," said Michael Berenbaum of the U.S. Holocaust Memorial Museum. Opened in 1993 as a monument to remembrance, it is dedicated to presenting the history of the persecution and murder of six million Jews as well as millions of homosexuals, gypsies, Jehovah's Witnesses, communists, Poles, and Catholics, all victims of Nazi tyranny.

The stories that are told throughout the four exhibit floors of the Holocaust Museum are of a personal nature: family photographs on display depict a whole town that was eradicated; personal items confiscated by the Nazis lay in piles: shoes, hairbrushes, sewing scissors, kitchen utensils; and the voices of victims recount their tales of horror in recorded interviews. Propaganda movies of the era and Nazi military film footage depict unspeakable inhumanity. Even the museum building was designed to create an uncomfortable feeling: it seems off-kilter, askew, twisted, and disorienting. "I wanted to convey the feeling of constantly being watched, of things closing in," explained architect James Freed. It is "horrible by design."

The study of world history teaches that events of the past hold moral lessons for future generations. The Holocaust was a racist outburst in which a civilized nation abused its powers, brutally violated human rights, and systematically engaged in the murder of millions. This museum provides an opportunity to consider how individual moral decisions can have far-reaching implications for the future. Unlike so many other museums, the U.S. Holocaust Museum does not celebrate human achievement; instead, according to its directors, it documents "a perversion of civilization [and] fosters an awareness of the consequences for all nations when mutual tolerance disappears."

Opposite page: The Tower of Faces (the Yaffa Eliach Shtetl Collection) in the Permanent Exhibition at the U.S. Holocaust Memorial Museum. Courtesy of the USHMM.

Guardians of Art and Sculpture: Galleries and Gardens

National Gallery

WEST BUILDING

"Noble in proportion, sober in elevation, supple in plan, elegant in materials, exemplary in detail," wrote architectural critic Benjamin Forgey of the West Building of the National Gallery of Art. Both the building and the collection can be attributed to the visionary foresight of Andrew W. Mellon.

Arriving in Washington from Pittsburgh in 1921, Mellon served through three administrations as secretary of the U.S. Treasury. His grandfather was from Ireland and settled in Pittsburgh in 1817, where he became a successful banker. Mellon took over the bank in 1882 and carefully invested his inherited fortune in coal, steel, street railways, and in Gulf Oil and Alcoa. Eventually he became one of the richest men in America, after John D. Rockefeller and Henry Ford.

Mellon paid millions in hard currency to the Soviet government in 1930 and 1931 to acquire many old masters' paintings from the Hermitage Collection. The famous British art dealer Lord Duveen sold Mellon numerous additional pieces, including Raphael's *Alba Madonna*, which became the nucleus of the National Gallery's collection.

In 1937 Mellon gave the nation 125 masterpieces from his collection of Western art, including works by Titian, Rembrandt, El Greco, and Botticelli, along with the funds for the construction of the West Building and a generous endowment. This was the largest gift that an individual had ever given to the government. Mellon was a brilliant businessman, so he arranged for a unique administrative structure to oversee the gallery: the federal government covers operating expenses while an independent, nine-member board of trustees manages the collection and programs, and only private donations are used for new acquisitions.

The site for the new gallery was chosen by Mellon, as was the building's architect, John Russell Pope. Mellon personally worked on the vast building's design, but specified that the new gallery was not to be named for him because, he said, no one would ever give money to a "Mellon Museum." The West Building has been described as being "among Washington's most elevating works of architecture," reaffirming Pope and Mellon's conviction that the design of public buildings in a democracy should be classical in style. Mellon and Pope died within a day of one another in August of 1937. The National Gallery of Art, opened in 1941, is their joint legacy to the nation and is now the most visited art museum in America.

Previous page:
David Smith, Cube XXVI, 1965, National Gallery of Art, Sculpture Garden.

National Gallery

EAST BUILDING

"Modest and kind, he was one of the greatest philanthropists of our time and a gentleman in every sense," said Earl "Rusty" Powell III, director of the National Gallery of Art, about Paul Mellon, the guiding spirit of the National Gallery and the man who turned it into one of the greatest art institutions in the world.

Paul Mellon supervised the construction of the West Building of the National Gallery after the death of his father, Andrew W. Mellon, in 1937 and served 47 years on the Board of Trustees. In the late 1960s he selected the architect I. M. Pei to design the new East Building and paid most of the cost of $100 million himself. Completed in 1987, the American Institute of Architects has named the East Building one of the ten best buildings in America.

The building is unique, modern, and monumental—yet still human in scale because of Pei's belief that the soul of architecture lies in geometry. Working with a difficult trapezoidal site, Pei ingeniously and elegantly divided it into two dissimilar triangles along the diagonal. The larger of the triangles is the part of the gallery devoted to the exhibition of art, while the smaller is devoted to scholarship. The apex of the smaller triangular portion of the building has a "knife-edge" angle of 19.5 degrees—the sharpest corner of any building in the world.

Pei understood that architecture needs art, so he commissioned many great artists to create works for the building. Alexander Calder created the colorful, 980-pound hanging, revolving mobile that fills the building's atrium; Pei later commented: "I can't imagine this space without it."

In his lifetime Paul Mellon gave more than 900 works of art to the National Gallery, and through his will left the Gallery $75 million and 100 additional works of art. Mellon was a famously modest philanthropist who enjoyed giving money away more than making it. Journalist Sarah Booth Conroy once wrote: "Mellon seems to buy what he likes and to enjoy spending his inheritance on sharing his passions with the rest of America." Not only did he make the National Gallery great, he gave the place its soul.

Typewriter Eraser, Sale X, Claes Oldenburg and Coosje van Bruggen, 1999.

National Gallery
SCULPTURE GARDEN

A "park-like museum—or museum-like park" describes the dual nature of the National Gallery of Art's Sculpture Garden. It isn't just about art: the sculpture garden contains nearly 100 varieties of trees, including cedars, cypress, magnolias, and dogwoods, as well as perennial flowers and carefully chosen shrubbery.

The 6½-acre sculpture garden is also a park within a park. The natural-style landscaping is reminiscent of the Mall in the 1850s, when it still featured Andrew Jackson Downing's Pleasure Gardens in front of the Smithsonian Castle. The similarity is not by happenstance: the idea was to create "a little echo of what got wiped out," explained landscape architect Laurie Olin, who designed the park with paths winding around a central circular pool with fountain, which serves as an ice-skating rink in the wintertime.

Marvelous late twentieth-century modern sculpture is carefully placed so as not to compete with the natural beauty of the garden. In one corner of the park is Claes Oldenburg's 20-foot-tall *Typewriter Eraser*; on the opposite side stands one of Barry Flanagan's comical rabbits, *Thinker on a Rock*; and scattered in between are many other pieces, including Isamu Noguchi's *Great Rock of Inner Seeking*, Roy Lichtenstein's transforming *House I*, Louise Bourgeois' towering bronze *Spider*, and Alexander Calder's delightful *Cheval Rouge*.

The first proposal for a sculpture garden on the Mall came in the 1960s; by 1974 the circular pool and ice-skating rink were built, but the surrounding area was barren, devoid of both plant life and sculpture. Thirty years later, through a generous donation from the Morris and Gwendolyn Cafritz Foundation, the garden was finally designed and completed. The National Gallery of Art's Sculpture Garden is "a fitting tribute to my parents, their love of Washington, and love for the visual arts," said Calvin Cafritz. It is "a place of quiet beauty."

Smithsonian

FREER GALLERY OF ART

"Touring the Freer Gallery of Art is like taking a trip around the world, and a trip through time," wrote journalist Carolyn Damstra. Charles Lang Freer was a self-made man: a Detroit railroad car manufacturer with a seventh-grade education whose accumulated wealth allowed him to retire at the age of 45. He spent two decades acquiring the world's finest art objects—dating all the way back to 1550 BC—a collection that he donated to the Smithsonian Institution in 1906.

Acclaimed for its rarity, authenticity, and the quality of its objects, the Freer Gallery has set high standards for Asian art collections. As the first American to collect certain non-Western objects, Freer always searched for the finest examples of art representing the cultures of Islam, India, China, Japan, and Korea. He believed that certain works of art from around the world shared common elements and were universally important as beautiful objects.

Freer's inspiration to collect Asian art came through his friendship with expatriate artist James McNeil Whistler. He believed Whistler was "the greatest figure of the nineteenth century in the broad field of the Fine Arts," that he bridged the divide between Eastern and Western art. Certain artists were kindred spirits, he thought, regardless of the physical distance or lifetimes that separated them.

Whistler's famous Peacock Room is part of Freer's collection that includes 1,234 of Whistler's paintings, etchings, and prints—the most comprehensive Whistler collection in the world. Childe Hassam, Winslow Homer, John Singer Sargent, Abbott H. Thayer, and Augustus St. Gaudens were among Freer's favorite American artists, and he purchased more than 200 paintings from them. He truly felt that they were "independently and unintentionally . . . continuers of the early Oriental ideal."

The Freer Gallery reflects the founder's taste and personality as few other art galleries do. In designing his museum, Freer wanted to create an ideal setting; he wanted others to enjoy his art in a "harmonious and contemplative atmosphere." Charles Lang Freer left many legacies: his gallery, his pursuit of excellence in collecting, and an inspiring example of how an individual can thoroughly educate himself. In describing what he learned from studying Freer's talents, one of the gallery's directors advised: "Train your eye, and if you see things that are really wonderful, collect them."

Smithsonian

SACKLER GALLERY

"I don't believe that there can be any creativity without passion . . . science is a discipline pursued with passion; art is a passion pursued with discipline . . . art and science are two sides of the same coin," explained Dr. Arthur M. Sackler. He described himself as physician, medical researcher, and publisher. Others say he was a man with an eye for art and a passion for collecting it. In 1987 Sackler gave nearly 1,000 Asian masterworks from his collection—one of the largest private collections of its type in the world—to the Smithsonian Institution, thereby establishing the Sackler Gallery of Art.

Sackler had studied art, but explained that when he realized that he couldn't create, he began to collect. He acquired his art in bulk and never sold anything from his collection. Sackler once explained that he collected art scientifically, "as a biologist." He asserted that to "really understand a civilization or a society, you must have a large enough corpus of data. You can't know twentieth-century art by looking only at Picassos and Henry Moores."

Sackler amassed a fortune through medical publications and advertisers. He was a self-made publishing magnate who had a fascination with creativity and wrote and spoke extensively on the psychological, biological, and social paths related to creativity.

His collection of ancient Chinese bronzes, dating from 1500 BC, provided him a glimpse into humanity, he said, recognizing that the bronze-caster's work combined an intuitive artistic awareness with skill and technology. It was "a triumphant demonstration of how one people can speak to all people: how artists can speak to everyone across the void of time . . . [and] how a past civilization can relate to the present through the power of its art. . . ." He was convinced that "[g]reat art doesn't belong to anybody. Never did. Never will. The more successful your collections are, the more they cease to be your property."

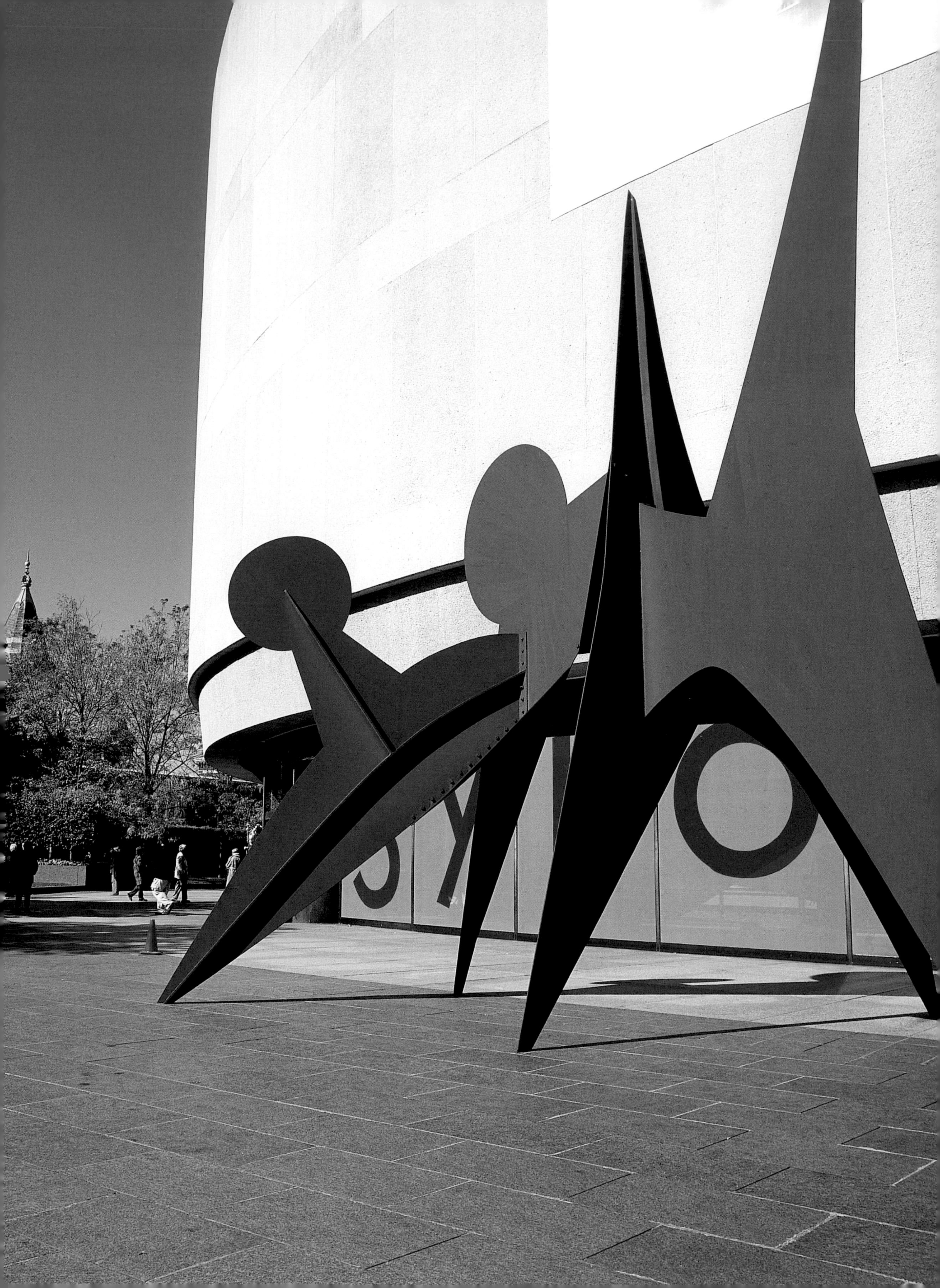

Smithsonian

HIRSHHORN MUSEUM AND SCULPTURE GARDEN

"I could not have done what I did in any other country. My collection belongs here," said Joseph Hirshhorn, referring to his fulfillment of the American dream. The twelfth child of a widowed Jewish immigrant was raised in squalid poverty in Brooklyn, yet by the age of 28 he was already a millionaire.

Hirshhorn amassed one of the most comprehensive collections of modern sculpture in the country, as well as an enormous collection of contemporary paintings and prints. Acquiring in bulk, Hirshhorn expanded his collection from 1,200 objects in 1957 to 6,000 in 1966: an average increase of more than one piece per day.

Hirshhorn's 1966 bequest to the Smithsonian Institution was very controversial: his reputation apparently clashed with the "sanctity of the Mall" and his taste in art was anything but conventional. The criticism extended to architect Gordon Bunshaft's design for the museum building: the donut-shaped, 82-foot-tall, cast-concrete cylinder was described as "brutal."

After the museum opened in 1974, however, public opinion changed. A sculptural statement in itself, the building's interior offers a brilliant double-ring plan, placing paintings in the windowless outer ring under artificial light and the sculpture in the window-lined, sunlight-filled inner ring.

Many critics noted that Hirshhorn had a better eye for sculpture than canvas, that he preferred objects he could touch. His sculpture collection, dating from the late nineteenth to mid-twentieth century, is one of the most highly acclaimed collections in the world and possibly the largest ever acquired by a single individual. In the Hirshhorn Sculpture Garden, as in the Hirshhorn Museum, unexpected, odd objects create an atmosphere of constant surprise. The abstract sculptures by Henry Moore, Alexander Calder, and Henri Matisse strongly contrast with August Rodin's emotional *Burghers of Calais*, the 1930 sculpture that memorialized the nineteenth-century heroes of Calais even as it heralded in the era of modern sculpture.

Monumental sculpture had traditionally been academic and allegorical, a means of commemorating great religious or political events. Joseph Hirshhorn recognized that large-scale sculpture was no longer constrained by limits on subject matter, scale, or space in the twentieth century. The Hirshhorn Sculpture Garden, with its variety of modern, monumental twentieth-century masterpieces, presents a "sensitive integration of art with its setting."

After the 1966 bequest, Hirshhorn donated another 1,000 pieces to the collection before handing over 5,300 final gifts just before his death in 1981. His greatest gift, however, might be the unusual freedom Hirshhorn granted the museum to sell or trade anything in the collection for other works of art—certainly the gift most appreciated by those who least appreciated Hirshhorn.

Mark Di Suvero, Are Years What? (for Marianne Moore), 1967.

Smithsonian

RENWICK GALLERY

"Dedicated to Art" is the inscription carved over the entryway of the Renwick Gallery. Established in 1859 and called the Corcoran Gallery after its founder, this was the largest building erected as a gallery of art in the United States at the time. It was "to be used solely for the purposes of encouraging American genius."

William Wilson Corcoran was a businessman, a banker, and Washington's greatest nineteenth-century philanthropist. He began collecting art in the 1840s when he purchased Hiram Powers' stunning marble sculpture entitled *Greek Slave*. Architect James Renwick was commissioned by Corcoran to design an art gallery with an octagonal room in which to showcase the beautiful statue. The octagonal gallery which was added to the Louvre in 1853 to display the Venus de Milo may have served as the inspiration for Corcoran's request; in fact, the "American Louvre" is the name some people gave to Corcoran's gallery.

The handsome building, designed in the French Second Empire style, was unfortunately not always used to display art. In 1861, even before it was completed, the government annexed the gallery for use as office space and for the storage and dispensing of army clothing and documents during the Civil War. Eventually the building was returned to Corcoran, who restored and reopened it, then donated the gallery to the public in 1874. In less than 25 years, the collection outgrew the space and had to be moved to a newly built gallery nearby.

For the next 65 years the gallery was occupied by the U.S. Court of Claims. In the 1960s it was declared to be "a crumbling eyesore and a firetrap" and the government resolved to tear it down. The original architectural drawings and photographs, still on file at the Library of Congress, were retrieved, and public and private interests united to save this important, historic national treasure from imminent destruction.

President Kennedy suggested transferring the gallery to the Smithsonian Institution to become a division of the Museum of American Art. In 1972 the gallery was reopened and renamed for the architect who designed it. On display are American crafts, including objects made of glass, clay, fiber, wood, and metal. Many of the one-of-a-kind works of art in the Renwick Gallery can be described as objects from everyday life turned fanciful by skill and imagination and, as Corcoran would say, by "American genius."

Smithsonian

NATIONAL MUSEUM OF AFRICAN ART

"The word got out . . . there was a crazy guy with an African art collection who had never been to Africa," explained Warren Robbins, founder of the National Museum of African Art. Robbins bought his first piece of African art for $15 in the 1950s while serving as a foreign service officer in Germany. A decade later he returned to Washington with hundreds of African items.

An idealist, Robbins hoped to find a way to help bridge the racial gap in America and to make a contribution of his own that would advance the cause of civil rights; he saw an opportunity to do so through art. "I had an admittedly quixotic vision," said Robbins, "that there should be in this nation (and appropriately in its capital) a museum dedicated exclusively to what had been the non-recognized, non-understood, and therefore non-valued cultural antecedents of that one-tenth of America's multi-ethnic population that traces its ancestry, in part, to Africa."

In 1964 Robbins opened the first museum in the country that promoted the

artistic heritage of Africa in a house on Capitol Hill—once the residence of former slave and abolitionist Frederick Douglass. Robbins eventually raised enough money to maintain a staff of 20 people and to expand the collection to 5,000 objects, which he housed in nine connected townhouses and a carriage house.

By the early 1980s, realizing that a permanent organization should oversee his collection, Robbins transferred his art to the Smithsonian Institution, which opened the National Museum of African Art in 1987. Merged together with Robbins' generous collection were thousands of African art objects that had been donated to the Smithsonian by hundreds of private collectors. The collection includes textiles, jewelry, masks, decorative arts, and architectural elements, placing unusual emphasis on utilitarian objects because—unlike Western art that is preserved and admired from a distance—in Africa, life and art are inseparable.

Corcoran Gallery of Art

Frank Lloyd Wright declared the "new" Corcoran Gallery of Art "the best designed building in Washington." The first Corcoran art gallery was located in William W. Corcoran's private home, which he opened to visitors twice a week. His prize possession, a nude sculpture called *Greek Slave,* so shocked Washingtonians that Corcoran invited men and women to view it separately.

The popularity of his collection inspired the generous philanthropist to construct a public building for the display of his artwork. The first Corcoran Gallery of Art (now called the Renwick Gallery) opened in 1874 with 98 paintings and sculptures. So many art students flocked to the gallery that a local painter volunteered free formal art instruction to those who were interested. Corcoran then donated funds "for the specific purpose of aiding in the establishing of a school of design." The Corcoran School of Art officially opened in 1890.

The collection and the school soon became overcrowded. The board of

trustees hired architect Ernest Flagg to design a new building in the Beaux-Arts style nearby, which he completed in 1897. Flagg designed a grand hall called the Hemicycle Gallery that was a semicircular, glass-roofed chamber measuring 1,850 square feet. Two stories tall, it was modeled after a similar two-story space in Paris' Ecole des Beaux-Arts. To Flagg's chagrin, it was later divided in half to create an upper and lower gallery. The upper gallery became Corcoran's chief venue for transitory shows; the gallery's first biennial exhibition of contemporary American painting was held there in 1915. The initial biennials attracted major American artists such as Edward Hopper and John Singer Sargent.

In 1925 Senator William A. Clark of Montana donated his extensive art collection to the Corcoran, including European paintings, sculptures, tapestries, stained glass, and the interior of an entire salon from the era of Louis XVI, "Le Salon Doré" from the Hotel d'Orsay in Paris. Ten years later, Edward and Mary Walker donated French impressionist works by Renoir, Monet, and Pissarro.

The board of trustees, though appreciative of such generous donations, generally restricts new purchases to works by American artists, because Corcoran stipulated that his gallery be for the encouragement of American genius. A senator noted in 1873: "If all the great capitalists that our country contains could be persuaded to imitate [Corcoran's] noble example, our republic would so become a paradise."

Smithsonian National Museum of American Art and National Portrait Gallery ©Smithsonian Institution.

Smithsonian

NATIONAL MUSEUM OF AMERICAN ART/ NATIONAL PORTRAIT GALLERY

Tending to wounded soldiers during the Civil War, the great American poet Walt Whitman described the makeshift hospital once called the Old Patent Office as "the noblest of Washington buildings." A century later that same noble edifice would become home to both the National Museum of American Art and the National Portrait Gallery.

Built between 1836 and 1867, the Patent Office was intended to be "a temple to the industrial arts" at a time when inventiveness was considered uniquely American. In its wide halls, patent models were proudly displayed alongside historic and scientific artifacts. On its walls hung the first federal art collection of privately donated paintings, and its rooms were decorated by the finest American sculptures.

The Patent Office's collection of American art was transferred to the Smithsonian Institution in 1858. More than a century later the Smithsonian acquired the building as well, filling its halls once again with that proud collection. Gilbert Stuart's colonial portraits, Mary Cassatt's impressionist paintings, Albert Bierstadt's landscapes, and Edward Hopper's twentieth-century realism are all present there today. The National Museum of American Art's collection of 50,000 works of art, spanning a period of more than 300 years, is the largest collection of its type in the world.

Also located in the Old Patent Office Building is the National Portrait Gallery. Portraits of heroes, villains, inventors, writers, and philosophers bring our nation's history alive through the power of painting, drawing, and sculpture. "Reading a portrait is in a way just as demanding as reading a text," said a former director of the portrait gallery. "It can also be an immediate and human experience."

"There came a time when sorrow almost overwhelmed me. Then I turned to my love of painting for the will to live." Duncan Phillips sought to overcome his grief over the deaths of his father and brother by bringing joy to his community. In 1921 the Phillips Memorial Gallery became the first gallery in the country dedicated to modern art.

The serene little gallery—three rooms in Phillips' mother's home—revolutionized Washington's art scene; for decades it was the only place in town where modern European and American art could be viewed.

In 1923 Phillips, heir to a banking and steel fortune, acquired Renoir's *Luncheon of the Boating Party* in Paris for $125,000. Despite the exorbitant price, Phillips rejoiced in the work that became the centerpiece of his collection, rightly predicting that "people will travel thousands of miles to our house to see it."

Phillips would only purchase a piece if he loved it. Whether newer pieces by Bonnard, Cezanne, or Georgia O'Keeffe, or older works by artists considered modern only in their own time, Phillips' only criterion was that the painting bring him joy by helping him to create "a haven for those who enjoy getting out of themselves and into the land of artists' dreams."

Sacred Structures: Saving Our Souls

St. John's Church on Lafayette Square

"I have just completed a church that made Washingtonians religious who had not been religious before," wrote architect Benjamin Henry Latrobe. First Lady Dolley Madison encouraged the city's prominent citizens to purchase the property for a new church opposite the White House. When St. John's Church was dedicated in 1816, it immediately became a gathering place for members of Washington's high society.

Membership in the church was by invitation only and the auction of pews provided the church's main source of income. When the elite members of Washington society rushed to buy pews, the church became known as the "Church of the Establishment," the "Church of the Diplomats," and the "Church of the Presidents," because Pew 28 was permanently reserved for the president.

A unique pulpit on wheels was installed, set on iron tracks in the brick floor to permit shifting it from the front to the center of the church according to the size of the congregation in attendance. Bishop Ravencroft enjoyed telling the tale of how, one Sunday while standing in the pulpit, "conscious of the distinguished and notable audience before me, and preaching to them with vigorous earnestness . . . of a sudden I felt the pulpit beneath me to be gliding away. Faster and faster towards the side wall of the church it was moving, and gaining rapidly as it went. The congregation were [*sic*] agitated; I was helpless; and I assure you I was considerably out of countenance when we stopped suddenly, and with a bump at the end of our notable journey." The pulpit was replaced with a stationary one.

Originally the church was designed and built in the form of a Greek cross and topped with a saucer-shaped dome pierced by semilune windows. In 1822 the church was enlarged to increase revenue: the west transept was extended and a bell tower added. By the 1870s a proposal was made to tear down the little church and replace it with a much larger, imposing, Victorian-style edifice.

The congregation, however, had second thoughts on the matter and decided instead to promote George Washington's earlier idea of building a grand church for national purposes in the city. They pioneered the fundraising efforts that resulted in the eventual construction of the Washington National Cathedral. St. John's remains unchanged on Lafayette Square across from the White House and still proudly bears its nickname "Church of the Presidents."

Previous page: Washington National Cathedral.

NO
STANDING
NO
PARKING
ENTRANCE

Washington National Cathedral

"Nobody here will live to see the completion of this cathedral," noted Bishop Satterlee as President Theodore Roosevelt laid the cornerstone of the Washington National Cathedral in 1907. He was proven wrong in 1990, when several people who were present that day as small children witnessed the placement of the last stone of the Cathedral.

The idea of building a cathedral in Washington was as old as the city itself. In 1791 the city's planner, L'Enfant, wrote of erecting a great church for national purposes that would be equally open to all. George Washington liked the idea, but under the American Constitution no church could be built by the government.

In 1893 Congress granted a charter to the Protestant Episcopal Cathedral Church of St. Peter and St. Paul. Funds were privately raised, architects chosen, plans drawn, the ground was broken, and by 1912 the first chapel was built. A young architect named Herbert Frohman, who visited the cathedral early in its construction, made a note in the visitors' book that he wished he might someday serve as the cathedral's architect. In 1921 the architectural firm for which he worked was contracted for the project and Frohman dedicated the rest of his life to the job.

As one of the best-known churches in the nation, the cathedral is considered "a house of prayer for all peoples" and everyone is invited to attend any of the 1,600 services offered there each year. Many famous preachers, including Billy Graham, Martin Luther King, Jr., and the Dalai Lama, have spoken from the cathedral's pulpit, and notables such as Woodrow Wilson, Admiral George Dewey, and Helen Keller are buried at the National Cathedral.

Built entirely of stone carved by hand, a thousand artisans worked throughout the twentieth century to create this great edifice of tall towers, flying buttresses, and massive columns that support the 100-foot-high vaulted ceilings. More than 100 carved gargoyles and 300 angels decorate the cathedral's exterior. Iconography in mosaics, needlepoint, wood, stone, and stained glass glorify both religious figures and American heroes alike. A moon rock brought back from the *Apollo 11* space mission was installed in one of the 200 stained-glass windows that bring dapples of brilliant color to the church's interior, prompting the chief stone mason, Joe Alonzo, to declare: "This building is one big work of art."

Basilica of the National Shrine of the Immaculate Conception

Called "America's Tribute to Mary," the National Shrine of the Immaculate Conception is a gift from all Catholics to the nation. Dedicated in 1959, the shrine is considered a place of pilgrimage for Catholics, just as America became a place of refuge for Catholic immigrants from all over the world. A belief in the Virgin Mary's central role in the Catholic Church led the first Catholic bishop of the United States, John Carroll, to declare Mary the protector of the new nation in 1792. Fifty-five years later Pope Pius IX proclaimed Mary the patroness of the United States.

Official sanction was given in 1914 for a great church dedicated to the country's patron saint to be built on the campus of the Catholic University. The cornerstone was laid in 1920; six years later the lower Crypt Church was completed and has been in constant use ever since. During the Depression years and World War II, construction was halted for lack of funds but was resumed again in 1953. Completed in 1959, the National Shrine of the Immaculate Conception became the largest Catholic church in America, capable of accommodating as many as 6,000 worshippers.

The decorations of the shrine's interior consumed an entire marble quarry in Italy. In the north apse of the church the largest mosaic of Christ in the world, the work of artist Jan Rosen, was installed as a gift from an anonymous donor. The shrine's ornamented exterior depicts, among other things, the founding of Maryland and of Christopher Columbus' discovery of America from the flagship *Santa Maria*.

Many of the church's 60 chapels dedicated to Mary were gifts from America's multiethnic Catholic community that reflect their immigrant roots. There are chapels dedicated to "Our Lady of Guadalupe," "Our Lady of Lourdes," "Our Lady of Czestochowa," "Our Lady of Siluva," "Our Lady of Fatima," and "Our Lady of Africa." Recently the Chapel of Our Lady of Hope was dedicated, a donation from Mr. and Mrs. Bob Hope in honor of his mother, Avis. Bob Hope later joked that, had he been given his say, he would have named the chapel "Our Lady of Avis Hope."

A SHARING WITH CHRISTS
BREAD IS A SHARING WITH

Cathedral of St. Matthew the Apostle

St. Matthew is the patron saint of civil servants: of accountants, bookkeepers, bankers, tax collectors, customs officials, security guards, and stockbrokers. Originally a Jewish tax collector who was despised as an extortionist by Jews and gentiles alike, he became an apostle of Jesus Christ and, finally, a saint. Every autumn St. Matthew's Cathedral celebrates the "Red Mass," in which guidance is requested for civil servants in their professional conduct. Supreme Court justices and members of Congress, the cabinet, the diplomatic corps, and other government department employees faithfully attend the service.

In the early 1800s the only Catholic church in the city of Washington was St. Patrick's, which was overcrowded by the 1830s. Father William Matthews, pastor of St. Patrick's and "the parochial patriarch of Washington City proper," gave his house to be sold so that the funds could be used for the construction of a new church building. The new church, built near the White House and completed in 1840, was named St. Matthew's to honor both the saint and Father Matthews. By 1893, however, the little church was surrounded by commercial buildings.

The answer was a new, grand Byzantine Romanesque-style structure was built for St. Matthew's Church in the popular Dupont Circle neighborhood. Dedicated in 1913, it was designated a cathedral in 1939 and described as "one of the ecclesiastical masterpieces of the city." The church's interior is magnificent: above the main entrance is a mural depicting saintly and eminent individuals of the Americas, including Simon Bolivar, the South American liberator; Reverend John Carroll, America's first archbishop; Edward Douglas White, Supreme Court chief justice; and, of course, the Reverend William Matthews. A bust of Pope John Paul II is on display, commemorating his 1979 visit to Washington, and a memorial plaque set in marble before the main altar solemnly states: "Here rested the remains of President Kennedy at the requiem mass, Nov. 25, 1963, before their removal to Arlington where they lie in expectation of a heavenly resurrection."

Outdoor Beauty: Parks and Gardens

Rock Creek Park

"Perhaps, not another city in the Union," wrote naturalist John Burroughs in 1869, has "so much natural beauty and grandeur" as Washington. He was inspired by the charm of the surrounding woodland valley and rushing ancient waters of Rock Creek.

For thousands of years the area was treasured by Native Americans who quarried the valley for quartzite and soapstone, and throughout the early nineteenth century European settlers established small commercial mills along Rock Creek. A mill owned by Isaac Pierce, a Pennsylvania Quaker whose family continued to grind corn and grain there until 1897, still stands today. During the Depression, it was used to provide flour for government cafeterias.

During the Civil War the military constructed several forts on the hills above Rock Creek, clearing away trees that obstructed the strategic lookout. After President Lincoln's assassination, Congress proposed relocating the presidential residence to Rock Creek Valley in order to increase security and "healthfulness."

The White House was never relocated, but the resultant congressional study focused attention on the deplorable, polluted condition of Rock Creek. Not until 25 years later, though, did several influential Washingtonians successfully lobby Congress to set aside 1,700 acres of land for a public park. Rock Creek Park, one of the largest urban parks in the world, became the third national park created by Congress. President Theodore Roosevelt was often accompanied by French Ambassador Jules Jusserand on "point-to-point" walks through the park. On one occasion, the two men were about to go skinny-dipping in the creek when Roosevelt noticed Jusserand still wore his gloves: "In case we meet ladies" was the ambassador's excuse. In 1936 President Franklin D. Roosevelt dedicated the Jusserand Memorial Bench near old Pierce Mill in Rock Creek Park.

Previous page: Constitution Gardens.

The United States Botanic Garden

"Gardens are like children. They take a great investment of time to bring to maturity," explained Holly Shimizu, director of the U.S. Botanic Garden, one of America's most historic institutions. In the 1790s both Washington and Jefferson urged Congress to "collect, cultivate and distribute" various plants from this and other countries to bring diversity to the nation's crops.

In the 1840s Admiral Charles Wilkes sent to Washington 10,000 plant specimens that he had collected on his 87,000-mile voyage around the world. Seeds from the Wilkes collection were propagated, and Congress authorized the construction of a botanical conservatory on the Mall to house the plants. In 1867 a large, domed greenhouse was built on the Capitol lawn, but would undergo several renovations and relocations before taking on its present form. The plants on display "must be either from the Wilkes Expedition, educational, endangered, or a participant in seasonal programs."

Across the street from the conservatory is the Botanic Garden's park, featuring *Fire and Water* in the center, a fountain sold to Congress by Frederic Auguste Bartholdi in order to finance his next project, the Statue of Liberty. The elaborate allegorical fountain features three 11-foot-tall caryatids supporting a wide basin, with water flowing between what were once 12 flaming gas lamps. In 1877, when the fountain was installed in front of the Capitol, the gas lamps were electrified, making it one of the first public displays of outdoor electricity and a popular tourist attraction.

The Botanic Garden sits quietly at the foot of the Capitol and still charm and captivate all who visit. "We are a living plant museum," said Holly Shimizu. "This isn't a building, it's a glasshouse, a place for plants . . . to tell a story."

Smithsonian

GARDENS ON THE MALL

Of the barren land surrounding the Smithsonian museums, S. Dillon Ripley correctly predicted: "Someday it will be a beautiful garden." The transformation of the Smithsonian Mall into a horticultural showplace began in the 1970s. In 1988 the garden named for Mary Livingston Ripley was filled with perennials, annuals, and decorative grasses planted in serpentine flower beds and along winding paths.

Near the Natural History Museum is the Ninth Street Butterfly Habitat Garden, which showcases four environments that attract butterflies: backyards, meadows, wetlands, and woodlands. Across the Mall the Rose Garden overwhelms the senses.

Behind the Castle is the Enid A. Haupt Garden, named for the donor. Resting on the roof of the Smithsonian's underground quadrangle museum complex, the Enid Haupt Garden features three different themes: a Victorian embroidered parterre that dominates the square; a summer garden modeled on the Alhambra in Granada; and a spring and fall garden inspired by the Temple of Heaven in Beijing. All of the Smithsonian gardens share one thing in common, as one of the gardeners explained: "[T]he experience begins the minute you walk in."

Constitution Gardens and the Signers Memorial

Constitution Gardens is reminiscent of the early plans for the Smithsonian Mall Pleasure Gardens. Dedicated as a bicentennial project, the 52-acre park is located near the Washington Monument.

The project was an ambitious undertaking at the time: throughout the nineteenth century the property was a marshy, tidal flatland. After a long and arduous draining, it was appropriated by the rapidly expanding national government during World War I in order to erect more office buildings.

By 1976 the buildings were gone, and in their place sat a lake with a little island. Six years later the island became a memorial to the 56 courageous men who signed the Declaration of Independence: wealthy, educated men who risked their life and prosperity by their act.

The final sentence of the Declaration of Independence, by which the signers earned their immortality, is inscribed in stone at the entry to the Signers Memorial: "And for the support of the Declaration, with a firm reliance on the protection of divine Providence, we mutually pledge to each other our Lives, our Fortunes, and our sacred Honor."

Smithsonian

NATIONAL ZOOLOGICAL PARK

After the Civil War, the yard behind the Smithsonian Castle became the city's first zoo. Taxidermists used the living specimens there as models when creating exhibits for the Museum of Natural History. The first exhibits attracted thousands of tourists a day, curious to see the American bison—a vanishing breed—and other "exotic" and interesting animals from the American frontier.

Landscape architect Frederick Law Olmsted designed the 166-acre park following the natural contours of Rock Creek Valley. In 1889 the National Zoo was established and immediately hailed as a "city of refuge" for the nation's vanishing species. Ties were close with Barnum & Bailey Circus, which passed on the first elephants, lions, and even zookeepers to the zoo.

Initially the zoo focused on exhibiting as many exotic species as possible, but by the 1950s began to emphasize the management and conservation of species. This led to inbred animals and the establishment of an international "dating service" among zoos to solve the problem. In 1972 two pandas, Hsing-Hsing ("shining star") and Ling-Ling ("darling little girl"), were given as a gift to the zoo from the People's Republic of China. They lived until the 1990s. In 2000 two new pandas, Mei Xiang ("beautiful fragrance") and Tian Tian ("more and more"), arrived for a 10-year stay.

The zoo's most famous resident, however, was Smokey the Bear. The burned and frightened $4^1/_2$-pound cub was rescued from a New Mexico forest fire in 1950 and became a symbol to help educate Americans about the dangers of forest fires. Though he died in 1976, Smokey the Bear is still one of America's best-loved icons.

Dumbarton Oaks Gardens and Montrose Park

Their dream was to have "a country house in the city"; so, in 1920, Robert and Mildred Bliss bought Dumbarton Oaks Estate in Georgetown. Robert Woods Bliss was a career diplomat; Mildred was an heiress to the Fletcher's Castoria patent medicine fortune—and loved gardens. Steep slopes and old farm buildings filled much of the estate's original 50 acres, where Mildred envisioned creating a series of formal, European-style, year-round gardens. Like the gardens of ancient Rome, these were to be lived in as outdoor rooms for private family use or extensive entertaining.

Beatrix Farrand, who described herself as the product of "five generations of garden lovers," was commissioned by Mildred Bliss to design the gardens of Dumbarton Oaks. Her color schemes resembled an impressionist painting, with broad sweeps of color harmoniously flowing from one garden into the next, creating an atmosphere of natural calm and restfulness.

Described as a "chambered nautilus of gardens," the sequence begins near the house with the monochromatic green garden terraces used for entertainment. Only trees, grass, and ivy are featured, allowing the brightly colored dresses of women guests to take center stage. Nearby is the tiny, walled "Star Garden," decorated in tile with the constellations, where the Blisses often ate breakfast. Densely shaded terraces lead to open, sunlit spaces with bursts of graduated colors. A hillside orchard shimmers in spring with soft shades of fruit tree blossoms. A pebble garden, covered with a thin sheet of water, glistens with earthy colors.

In 1940 the Blisses divided the estate between

Harvard University and the National Park Service. The estate mansion became a research center with two libraries and a museum housing one of the world's finest Byzantine art collections, along with a major exhibit of pre-Columbian artifacts and objects that once belonged to Robert Woods Bliss.

Set into the east wall of the Bliss' favorite garden, the Rose Garden, are two escutcheons crowned by the Bliss family crest of a sheaf of wheat. Below is inscribed the family motto, *Quod Severis Metes* ("as ye sow, so shall ye reap"). Here rest the ashes of Robert and Mildred Bliss.

Montrose Park is a 16-acre park on the heights of Georgetown that has been a popular gathering place for more than 200 years. The property was burned by the British in 1814—the only significant damage done in Georgetown during the War of 1812. Fourth of July celebrations were held on the property, as was the city's first agricultural fair.

Montrose Park has had many names. Richard Parrott bought the land in 1804 and built a house there that he called "Elderalie," but the rope-making business that he ran on the site prompted others to call it "Parrott's Ropewalk." In 1837 the Boyce couple moved in and renamed the place "Montrose" after the Scottish earl from whom Captain Boyce was descended. When he died in 1858, Mrs. Boyce moved to England and thenceforth the house remained mostly vacant and fell into disrepair.

Toward the end of the nineteenth century, Sarah Louisa Rittenhouse began working with the women of Georgetown to secure the property for a public park. Miss Loulie, as she was known, had grown up at "Bellevue" (Dumbarton House) a few blocks away and remembered the picnics and grand events once held at Montrose. Years of letter writing to members of Congress finally proved successful.

In 1911 Montrose Park became part of the government-owned system of parks. The rose gardens, planted where the estate house once stood, were named Rittenhouse Gardens in honor of Miss Loulie. In 1956 the Georgetown Garden Club placed the bronze armillary sphere in the park in her memory.

Historic Preservation: Saving Our Past

Ford's Theatre and the Petersen House

Abraham Lincoln attended performances at Ford's Theatre eight times during the Civil War. Five days after the war ended, while he sat watching the benefit performance of *Our American Cousin*, an assassin's bullet took his life.

John T. Ford first opened his theatre in a vacant Baptist church in late 1861. For many Washington residents it became a popular place to escape from the realities of the war. On New Year's Eve 1862 a fire destroyed the church, but eight months later a new theater was opened on the same site.

Soon after the reopening, Lincoln attended a performance starring John Wilkes Booth, a popular stage performer from a distinguished family of actors. Booth was known to be an affected egotist, a narcissistic actor who craved dramatic immortality. By 1864 Booth believed Lincoln was a tyrant, responsible for all the troubles in the South, and he had plotted to kidnap the president and deliver him to Confederate territory. After Lee's surrender, however, he resolved to kill both the president and General Grant. With the aid of conspirators, he planned to also kill the vice president and secretary of state on the same night.

Previous page: French Drawing Room, Hillwood Museum.

The Grants did not accompany the Lincolns to Ford's Theatre, as originally expected, and so General Grant's life was spared. Secretary of State Seward, though grievously wounded, survived a near-fatal stabbing by one of Booth's associates. Vice President Johnson was saved when his assigned assassin got drunk.

After shooting the president, Booth escaped from the theatre, but Union soldiers eventually caught up with him 12 days later. Found hiding in a barn, Booth taunted the soldiers and they shot him; he died a few hours later. Seven conspirators were tried and convicted for the abduction and assassination plot against the president; four were hanged, the other three received life sentences.

Ford's Theatre was closed and the building was sold to the government for office use. In 1893, 23 office workers were tragically killed in the building when the overloaded floors collapsed. In 1932 a small Lincoln museum was opened in part of the old theatre. In 1968 the building was fully restored not only as a museum but also as a center for contemporary American theater.

Across the street from Ford's Theatre is a boarding house where the mortally wounded president was carried the night he was shot. The next morning, Lincoln died in the back bedroom of Mr. Petersen's Boarding House. The ordinary Washington row house owned by William Petersen became famous as "the house where Lincoln died." Most tenants soon moved out, and after Mr. and Mrs. Petersen both died in 1871, the furnishings—including Lincoln's deathbed—were auctioned to help settle the estate debts, and finally the house itself was sold. In 1896 the government purchased the house but did not open it to the public until 1932. The Petersen House has been called the city's most modest museum.

Presidential Box, Ford's Theatre.

Room where President Lincoln died on April 15, 1865, Petersen House.

Old Post Office Tower

Even before its completion in 1899, the Old Post Office Tower was already described as hideous and old-fashioned by architects and the general public. Both the city and federal post offices vacated the premises; demolition was postponed only by the financial inability to replace it. Other government offices were housed in the neglected edifice until 1975, when it was suggested that the building be razed.

The building did have some redeeming qualities, however, and protestors drew attention to them as features of historical and architectural value to Washington in 1971. Eventually the chairperson of the National Endowment for the Arts, Nancy Hawks, convinced Congress to pass the Public Buildings Act in 1976, rendering all government buildings potentially profitable through private investment. These two events managed to save the Old Post Office once and for all.

A British-American Friendship foundation donated a gift of 10 change-ringing bells for the clock tower. They are rung for opening and closing sessions of Congress and on national holidays.

Union Station

In 1908 Union Station was hailed as "a monument to the progress of railroading and the art of traveling." Architect "General" Daniel Burnham designed a self-contained little city, a monumental gateway to the nation's capital that embodied his philosophy: "Make no little plans; they have no magic to stir men's blood."

Though grandiose at birth, in the 1950s the glory of Union Station began to fade: a runaway train crashed into the station in 1953; declining interest in train travel left the station neglected and attempts to draw back visitors failed; and severe water damage finally closed the station in 1981.

Nevertheless, the station was declared a national historical landmark in 1964, and in 1983 a loan from Amtrak combined with federal funds and private investment provided for renovations . . . and the little city was reborn.

Woodrow Wilson House

Immediately after President Harding's inaugural ceremonies, Woodrow Wilson and his second wife, Edith, left the White House and drove to their newly purchased home, where they would spend the rest of their lives. Built in 1915 by Boston businessman Henry Parker Fairbanks, the three-story, 28-room, neo-Georgian house in Washington's premier neighborhood was described by Edith as "an unpretentious, comfortable, dignified house suited to the needs of a gentleman."

Thomas Woodrow Wilson, the son of a Presbyterian minister, was the only president to earn a Ph.D. In 1890 Princeton offered him a professorship and later elected him president. In 1910 Wilson was elected governor of New Jersey, but served only one term before being elected twenty-eighth president of the United States.

"The world must be made safe for democracy," declared Wilson as he carried America into World War I. At the war's end, he helped draw up the terms of peace and worked valiantly to establish the League of Nations. While trying to rally support for his peace efforts, he overextended himself and suffered a stroke.

Just three years after moving into their new home, President Wilson died and his body was taken to the Washington National Cathedral, where it lies entombed in the nave. Edith stayed in the house until her death in 1961; she had specified that, after her death, the house should be presented to the American people under the guardianship of the National Trust for Historic Preservation, and her will was done.

Tudor Place

Once a center for Washington's intellectual and cultural elite, the architectural and historical integrity of Tudor Place was preserved as a sacred trust by six generations—178 years—of a single family. Martha Curtis Peter, granddaughter of Martha Washington, and Thomas Peter, the son of the first mayor of Georgetown, purchased $8^{1}/_{2}$ acres of land in the heights of Georgetown in 1805. Dr. William Thornton, architect of the Capitol and family friend, designed the mansion, and Martha brought to the house a priceless collection of Washington family memorabilia.

Their daughter Brittania was mistress of the house from her mother's death in the 1850s until her own death in 1911. While there, she carefully documented the home's contents and even saved them and the house itself from ruin during the Civil War when she volunteered Tudor Place for use as officers' quarters so that it would not become a hospital, as the government planned.

Ownership of the house passed to her grandson, Armistead Peter Jr., who in turn left it to his son, Armistead Peter, III, founder of the Tudor Place Foundation. The foundation is responsible for preserving the house and gardens, which it opened to the public in 1988.

Hillwood Museum & Gardens

She was called "the American Empress," and her home was affectionately referred to as "Moscow on the Potomac" and "Washington's Little Versailles." In 1955 the 68-year-old Marjorie Merriweather Post purchased the lavish 25-acre estate named Hillwood and transformed it into a museum home where she lived and entertained for the remainder of her life.

This treasure house of Washington is filled to overflowing with a vast decorative arts collection of approximately 6,000 items, chosen from an original collection many times that size. Marjorie inherited a fortune at just 27 years of age when her father, the inventor C. W. Post, died. As his only child, he trained her to take over the company that he created to promote and manufacture health foods.

When she became convinced that frozen foods could transform everyday life as well, she purchased Birds Eye Frozen Foods, the first in a series of food companies that Marjorie would acquire and merge to create what soon became the powerful General Foods Corporation.

A legendary heiress, Marjorie Merriweather Post was unpretentious, kind, and generous to all. She entertained Vietnam veterans, supported the American Red Cross and the Boy Scouts of America, donated jewels to the Smithsonian Institution, money to the Kennedy Center and the National Symphony Orchestra . . . and she gave her home to the American people.

Octagon House

Despite its name, Octagon House has only six sides and a rounded front bay. Designed by the Capitol's architect, Dr. William Thornton, and commissioned by Colonel John Tayloe III, Octagon House figured centrally in Washington's early social life. In 1814, after the British invaded Washington and set fire to the White House, Octagon House was offered to James and Dolley Madison for use as a temporary presidential residence. It was there that President Madison signed the Treaty of Ghent, ending the War of 1812.

In the 1890s the American Institute of Architects recognized the house's architectural and historical importance and undertook to renovate it. In 1970 Octagon House was designated a national historic landmark and opened to the public.

Blair-Lee House

Sometimes called the "nation's guest house," Blair-Lee House was designated the official residence for guests of state by Franklin Roosevelt. President Truman himself lived here for four years while the White House was under renovation. Built in 1824 by the nation's first surgeon general, Dr. Joseph Lovell, the house was sold just twelve years later to Francis Preston Blair. The home was then passed to his son Montgomery, who was President Lincoln's postmaster general, and finally to Montgomery's son Gist, who bequeathed the residence to the government in 1942, specifying that it should be preserved as a memorial to his family and the prominent role it played in the history of the country.

25

Outdoor Sculpture: Memorials to Heroes and Peacemakers

Philip Sheridan Statue

Inspired by Thomas Buchanan Read's poem "Sheridan's Ride," sculptor John Gutzon Borglum undertook to capture in bronze one of the Union's most celebrated cavalry heroes. Seated atop his spirited stallion, Rienzi, General Sheridan is depicted riding into Winchester in 1864 to send his frightened and retreating troops back into battle, where they soon won victory for the Union.

Best known for the fiery speeches he gave to rally his men into battle, Sheridan is posed as if addressing his troops. Dedicated in 1908, the magnificent statue established Borglum as one of America's foremost monument sculptors.

Previous page: Philip Sheridan Memorial.

Dupont Circle

Dupont Circle, one of seven circles that appeared on L'Enfant's original city plan, remained unnamed and undeveloped until after the Civil War, when a landscaping plan proposed planting 850 ornamental trees and shrubs there. In 1884 the circle was officially named Dupont Circle for Civil War admiral Samuel Francis du Pont, whose capture of Port Royal, South Carolina, was the first Union naval victory.

In 1921 a marble fountain by Daniel Chester French replaced an original—very unpopular—statue of du Pont. Dedicated to "the Arts of Navigation," it features three eight-foot-tall, allegorical statues representing the Stars, Winds, and Seas, and supporting the basin of flowing water.

The area was then neglected until, in the 1960s, it finally became a stage for anti-war demonstrations and a hangout for hippies and black-power advocates. When property values began to increase again in the 1970s, the area was declared to be of historic interest. Dupont Circle remains the most frequented neighborhood park in the city, inviting a diverse mix of people to play music, chess, or just to sit and watch the world go by.

Major General John A. Logan Statue

"The thirtieth of May, 1868, is designated for the purpose of strewing with flowers, or otherwise decorating the graves of comrades who died in defense of their country during the late rebellion." With these words General John Alexander Logan established "Decoration Day," later declared the national holiday Memorial Day.

When the Civil War broke out, Logan left his post as congressman to join the Union army and quickly rose through the ranks from colonel to general. After the war Logan became extremely popular among veterans: having returned to his place on Capitol Hill, he fought hard for pensions and benefits for the "boys in blue," and helped establish the Grand Army of the Republic, the principal organization for Union veterans. Upon his death in 1886, Union veterans and Logan's resolute widow raised funds for his memorial.

Sculptor Franklin Simmons was chosen to cast Logan's likeness in bronze. Simmons portrayed Logan seated atop his restless horse, chest puffed, shoulders back, and sword drawn, looking both brave and belligerent. The bronze pedestal features allegorical figures of War and Peace in bas-relief on the northern and southern faces, and two elaborate scenes on east and west: Logan presiding over a war council and his swearing-in ceremony at the Senate.

Hardly a visitor pays any attention to the historical inaccuracy of the scenes today, though they were very controversial at the time: Logan's widow insisted that her husband be represented at just these two events, but with all the great men with whom he served in different times and places. The memorial was placed in the center of Iowa Circle in 1901, renamed Logan Circle 30 years later.

Admiral Farragut Statue

Cast from the bronze propeller of Admiral David Glasgow Farragut's ship, the *USS Hartford*, Vinnie Ream's statue memorializes the Union hero who captured New Orleans and spoke the famous words, "Damn the torpedoes! Full speed ahead!" before destroying the Confederate navy.

Comte de Rochambeau Statue

This bold statue of Major General Comte de Rochambeau, who fought alongside General Washington in the Battle of Yorktown to end the Revolutionary War, features elements that pay tribute to both the lands that Rochambeau held in his heart: France and America.

Daniel Webster Statue

Presented to the government by the *Washington Post* founder Stilson Hutchins, the Daniel Webster Statue honors the rebellious statesman who proclaimed "Liberty and union—now and forever—one and inseparable" at the famous 1830 congressional "battle of the giants," depicted on the base.

José de San Martín Statue

José de San Martín, liberator of Argentina, Chile, and Peru, was called the George Washington of Spanish America. This replica of Augustin-Alexandre Dumont's original statue in Buenos Aires was given to the American people by the citizens of that city in 1925.

Ulysses S. Grant Memorial

Two prominently placed memorials, both dedicated in 1922, were designed to anchor the Mall: Lincoln's on the west end, Grant's on the east. Grant was the Union army's most important leader, to whom the salvation of the Union is ascribed together with President Lincoln.

Henry M. Shardy spent his entire career perfecting this one memorial and died two weeks before its dedication. Shady's design captured all the horrors of war, perhaps even too realistically for many visitors. Centered on a 252-foot-long marble plaza, an enormous General Grant sits atop his horse, slouched under his heavy cloak, staring intensely from beneath a weather-beaten hat, appearing calm amid the chaos around him: a weary artillery group whose horses are out of control, a horrified cavalry group that cannot avoid trampling a fellow soldier, and all the world rushing into battle regardless.

Mahatma Gandhi Monument

Sculpted by Gautam Pal, this memorial is inscribed only with the words "My life is my message," referring to the life of peaceful protest against immoral and unjust authority that changed not just India, but the entire world. Depicted on his "march to the sea," the man of action stands memorialized before the Indian embassy, but facing the British embassy.

Mary McLeod Bethune Memorial

The first Washington public memorial both to a woman and an African American, Capitol Hill's statue of Mary McLeod Bethune was sponsored by the National Council of Negro Women—which she founded—and sculpted by Robert Berks. The noble daughter of freed slaves reaches out to two children, symbolic of her life of dedication to the advancement of young African Americans.

Albert Einstein Memorial

By commission of the National Academy of Sciences, Robert Berks sculpted this impressionistic bronze statue of Einstein in 1979, the centennial of his birth. Standing atop a sky map on the Norwegian emerald-pearl base, the revolutionary scientist holds a page inscribed with three of his most important equations. At three times life-size, Einstein rightfully appears a giant among men.

George Mason Memorial

In the 10,000-square-foot garden that lies in the shadow of the Jefferson Memorial stands the nation's tribute to the "Father of the Bill of Rights": a bronze statue of a pensive George Mason seated on a stone bench. Though not as well-known as many of the Founding Fathers, Mason exerted tremendous influence over them. He disliked public politics himself and so remained in the background, but all the great men of the time knew him and sought his advice.

In 1776 Mason authored the Virginia Declaration of Rights, the country's first bill of rights and the basis for the constitutional amendment. In 1787 he was a Virginia delegate to the Philadelphia Convention that drafted the Constitution, but refused to sign the document because it failed to protect the rights of the individual citizen. Later that year, however, James Madison led Congress in amending the Constitution to include Mason's Bill of Rights.

Mason's political and philosophical ideas on human rights heavily influenced France's Declaration of the Rights of Man and the United Nations' Declaration of Human Rights, as well as early democratic reform movements throughout Europe and, of course, future generations.

© Orhan Çam

Martin Luther King, Jr. Memorial

"With this faith, we will be able to hew out of the mountain of despair a stone of hope," declared Martin Luther King Jr. in his "I Have A Dream" speech. This quote was the inspiration behind his memorial. The "Mountain" is located at the memorial's entrance, represented by two large granite masses; this leads to the "Stone," from which emerges a relief carving of King, looking contemplative and a little defiant.

A crescent-shaped black granite wall flanks the memorial, on which 14 quotes from King's speeches and sermons are inscribed. They reflect his beliefs in "hope and possibility . . . a future anchored in dignity, sensitivity and mutual respect." The earliest quote dates from the 1955 Montgomery, Alabama Bus Boycott; the last from his 1968 sermon delivered at the Washington National Cathedral.

King's roots were in the African American Baptist Church where his father and grandfather were pastors. He received a Ph.D. in systematic theology in 1955, and two years later, helped found the Southern Christian Leadership Conference. In 1963, King assisted in assembling mass civil rights demonstrations in Birmingham, Alabama, and became Time magazine's Man of the Year. The next year he received the Nobel Peace Prize.

The memorial, dedicated in 2011, was a 27-year long, $120 million project that unfortunately received startling criticism: Translating a metaphor into stone seemed trite; choosing a Chinese artist was un-American. King's statue was described as pseudo-monumental, Stalinist kitsch, and the "Mountain" was called cartoonish. Adding to the controversy, a prominently carved inscription misquoted King. One critic simply concluded ". . . monumental intentions have gone unfulfilled."

King, however, is the only private citizen to be honored with a national holiday and to have a major memorial on the National Mall. His legacy is his belief in the "American Dream"—of freedom, democracy, and opportunity for all.

Unusual Statues: Personal Expression

"Titanic" Memorial

Designed by Gertrude Vanderbilt Whitney and sculpted by John Horrington, this pink granite memorial with arms outstretched to form a cross was dedicated in 1931 to those "who gave their lives nobly to save women and children" in the 1912 sinking of the Titanic.

Temperance Memorial

In the late nineteenth century the eccentric millionaire Henry Cogswell attempted to cure widespread national drunkenness by donating ice-water fountains to cities across America. The Cogswell Memorial Temperance Fountain, inscribed with the words "Faith, Hope, Charity, and Temperance," is the only one left standing today.

Adams Memorial

"The whole meaning and feeling of the figure is in its universality and anonymity. My own name for it is 'the Peace of God,'" wrote Henry Adams. Not a portrait, nor allegorical, romantic, or religious and without inscription whatsoever, the Adams Memorial denied all past traditions of Western funeral art when it was placed in Rock Creek Cemetery in 1891.

Henry Adams, a distinguished historian and great-grandson of President John Adams, was devastated by the suicide of his wife, Clover, following a deep depression and mourning for her father. Six months after her death he left for the Orient, where he seemed to attain an inner peace through an understanding of the Buddhist concept of Nirvana. On his return, Adams contacted the artist Augustus Saint-Gaudens and began discussing plans for a genderless statue that would symbolize "the acceptance, intellectually, of the inevitable," and would "ask a question, not give an answer." The enigmatic, contemplative, shrouded bronze figure is considered Saint-Gaudens' masterpiece.

Higher Education:

George Washington University

Washington's first college was founded by the Baptist Church in 1819 on "College Hill," a rural tract of land north of the White House. Originally called Columbian College, it was renamed Columbian University after Washington philanthropist William Wilson Corcoran donated a block of downtown property to the school. The idea of an urban campus was born when the Medical Department first leased classroom space downtown. The expansion could not occur, however, until Corcoran's gift permitted "College Hill" to be sold after occupation by the Union army for use during the Civil War.

When a ladies' society, the George Washington Memorial Association, offered to finance construction on the newly purchased Van Ness estate, the University accepted their conditions that women be granted admission, and that the school be renamed the George Washington University.

Georgetown University

Georgetown University is the oldest university in Washington, the oldest Catholic college in the country, and the only Catholic school to have reached a status akin to an Ivy League school. In 1789 Reverend John Carroll founded the Jesuit-run "Academy on the Potomac" that was "open to students of every religious Profession," after having himself been refused entry to American colleges and imprisoned in Europe for joining the Jesuit Order.

Bishop Carroll secured a deed to 60 acres of land above the port of Georgetown. In 1795 the first building, Old North, was completed; in 1866 the school's official colors became blue and gray, symbolizing the reunification of North and South. Healy Hall, named for the Reverend Patrick Healy, the first black man in the United States to earn a Ph.D. and president of Georgetown College, is found in the National Register of Historic Places.

City of Learning

The Catholic University of America

In 1887 Mary Gwendoline Caldwell "founded" the Catholic University of America when she donated $300,000 to purchase Turkey Thicket, formerly the country estate of Margaret and Samuel Harrison Smith. The purchase fulfilled the dreams of American bishops who wanted to open up higher education to clergymen. The first students attended classes in St. Thomas Hall—the Smith's stucco cottage—in 1890. In 1914 the University rector obtained permission from the pope to build the National Shrine of the Immaculate Conception on campus.

The Catholic University of America is the only university in the United States chartered by the Vatican and the only one that answers directly to the Roman Catholic Church. Most faculties, however, are not bound by the charter, and the university openly welcomes students of all faiths.

Howard University

Two years after the Civil War, Congress chartered "a university for the education of youths in the liberal arts and sciences." Although the university's motto was "Equal Rights and Knowledge for All," Howard offered African Americans a quality education that they couldn't get anywhere else at the time. During segregation in the United States, Howard became a mecca for black intellectuals.

The school was named for Oliver Otis Howard, a war hero and civil rights advocate who became the school's third president. The first African American president, Mordecai Johnson, worked to obtain full accreditation for all the university's departments.

The Founder's Library contains one of the largest collections of materials documenting the history and culture of black people from Africa and the Americas. Howard's faculty is the largest assembly of African American scholars at any U.S. university, and the university hospital is the nation's only African American medical center.

Index